D0533558

BRADSHAW'S GUIDE TO BRUNEL'S RAILWAYS

Volume One:
Paddington to Penzance

John Christopher

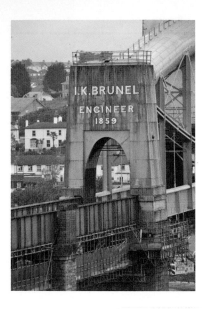

The eastern portal of the Royal Albert Bridge crossing the Tamar at Saltash to carry the line from Devon into Cornwall. It was a triumph of engineering on Isambard Kingdom Brunel's part, but he died later in the same year in which the bridge was completed. The wording was added as a tribute to the great man, and this photograph was taken in 2012 before the recent refurbishment had reached this part of the bridge.

About this book

This book explores many aspects of the railway journey from Paddington to Penzance. Through Bradshaw's text and the supportive images and information it describes the line, its main features and some of the many changes that have occurred over the years. Hopefully it will encourage you to delve a little deeper when exploring Brunel's railways and other works, but please note that public access and photography is sometimes restricted for reasons of safety and security.

First published 2013

Amberley Publishing
The Hill, Stroud
Gloucestershire, GL5 4EP

www.amberley-books.com

ISBN 978 1 4456 2159 3
ISBN EBOOK 978 1 4456 2165 4

Typeset in 9.5pt on 12pt Celeste.
Typesetting by Amberley Publishing.
Printed in the UK.

Bradshaw and Brunel

George Bradshaw and Isambard Kingdom Brunel had several things in common. They were close contemporaries who enjoyed considerable success in their chosen fields and both men died when relatively young. Bradshaw, born in 1801, died in 1853 aged fifty-two, while Brunel, born just a few years later in 1806, was fifty-three years-old when he died in 1859. In all likelihood they never met, but their names were drawn together by an unprecedented transport revolution which happened to take place during their brief lifetimes. It was Brunel and his fellow engineers who drove the railways, with their cuttings, embankments and tunnels, through a predominantly rural landscape to lay the foundations of the nineteenth century industrial powerhouse that has shaped the way we live today. The fallout from that revolution is frequently glossed over by the pageantry of the heritage business, as epitomised by Brunel's central role in the opening ceremony for the London 2012 Olympics, but there is no doubt that the railways brought distant towns and cities closer together in a way never seen before. They shrank space and time. Before their coming different parts of the country had existed in local time based on the position of the sun, with Bristol, for example, running ten minutes behind London. The Great Western Railway changed all that in 1840 when it applied synchronised railway time throughout its area.

The timing of the publication of Bradshaw's guidebooks is of particular interest. This account is taken from the 1863 edition which, of necessity, must have been written slightly earlier. We know that a continuous journey from London to Penzance wasn't possible until the opening of the Royal Albert Bridge in May 1859, and that the first trains to run all the way to Penzance did so the following year. So from this we can deduce that it was written within a relatively narrow time frame between 1860 and the end of 1862, or early 1863 at the latest. That was an extremely interesting time for the railway companies. The heady days of the railway mania of the 1840s were over and they had settled into the daily business of transporting people and goods. By the early 1860s the GWR's mainline from London to Bristol had been in operation for around twenty years and was still largely in its original as-built form. The quadrupling of the tracks between London and Didcot was a decade away and most of the GWR's constituent parts, such as the Bristol & Exeter Railway (B&ER), the South Devon Railway (SDR) and the two Cornish railways existed as separate entities, albeit engineered by Brunel to his chosen broad gauge. It was also by this time that rail travel had become sufficiently commonplace to create a market for Bradshaw's guides.

Isambard Kingdom Brunel and George Bradshaw

Two Victorians whose prosperity and fame grew with the rapid spread of Britain's railway network. Close contemporaries, they were born and also died only a few years apart, there is no record of them having met. *Below,* William Powell Frith's painting *The Railway Station* depicted a Great Western Railway broad gauge train about to depart from Platform 1 at Paddington station. Frith's narrative style caused a sensation when the painting was first put on display in 1862, just one year before *Bradshaw's Descriptive Railway Hand-Book* was published.

As a young man George Bradshaw had been apprenticed to an engraver in Manchester in 1820, and after a spell in Belfast he returned there to set up his own business as an engraver and printer specialising principally in maps. In October 1839 he produced the world's first compilation of railway timetables. Entitled *Bradshaw's Railway Time Tables and Assistant to Railway Travelling* the slender cloth-bound volume sold for sixpence. By 1840 the title had changed to *Bradshaw's Railway Companion,* the price doubled and it evolved into a monthly publication with the price returned to the more affordable sixpence. Although Bradshaw died in 1853 the company continued to produce the timetables and in 1863 launched *Bradshaw's Descriptive Railway Hand-Book of Great Britain and Ireland.* Originally published in four sections this was a proper guidebook without the timetable information of the monthly publications. Universally referred to as Bradshaw's Guide it is this publication that features in Michael Portillo's *Great British Railway Journeys,* and as a result has found itself catapulted into the best-seller list almost 150 years after it was originally published.

Without a doubt the guides were invaluable in their time and also provide the modern-day reader with a fascinating insight into the mid-Victorian rail traveller's experience. For example they sing the praises of the Devon countryside, yet dismiss Cornwall as 'one of the least inviting of the English counties'. At that time the Cornish railways principally served the needs of the mining and minerals industry and Bradshaw could not have predicted the rise in tourism that his guides helped to create. In 1865 *Punch* praised Bradshaw's publications, stating that 'seldom has the gigantic intellect of man been employed upon a work of greater utility'. Having said that, the facsimile editions available nowadays don't make easy reading with their close-set type. There are scarcely any illustrations, and attempts to trace linear journeys from A to B are interrupted by branch line diversions. It is also fair to say that Bradshaw's account is not written from an engineering perspective. While it describes many aspects of the route, in particular the physical features, stations and so on, there is no reference to the locomotives or major works, whereas the Eddystone Lighthouse is covered in great detail because it was of interest to the general reader.

That's where this volume comes into its own. *Bradshaw's Guide to Brunel's Railways, Volume 1,* takes you on a continuous journey from Paddington via Bristol all the way to Penzance in Cornwall. The locations of Bradshaw's diversions on the various branch lines are indicated in square brackets, but note that these are not described in order to maintain the flow of our journey. Additional information is provided on Brunel, his railways and many of the locations along the route. Naturally enough our journey through time commences at the greatest of Brunel's railway stations – Paddington!

Paddington station, London

Top: Interior of Paddington's wooden engine shed with central turntable. Designed by Daniel Gooch, the GWR's first 'Superintendent of Locomotive Engines', this innovative circular layout was much copied by other railway companies.

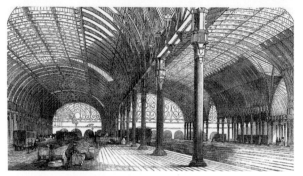

Middle: Engraving of Brunel's New Paddington station, a cathedral-like structure with three 700 foot-long transepts or spans of wrought iron and glass. Completed in 1854 this replaced a temporary station which had been located just beyond the Bishop's Road Bridge. The influence of Joseph Paxton's Crystal Palace for the Great Exhibition of 1851 is clear to see, which is hardly surprising as Brunel had sat on the exhibition building committee and the two men enjoyed a close working relationship.

Left: Paddington was a station without a frontage. That role was played by the Great Western Royal Hotel, designed by Philip Hardwick in the style of a French château.

Below: Detail from a 1920s GWR route map with the main line to Bristol heading westwards then curving upwards via Didcot.

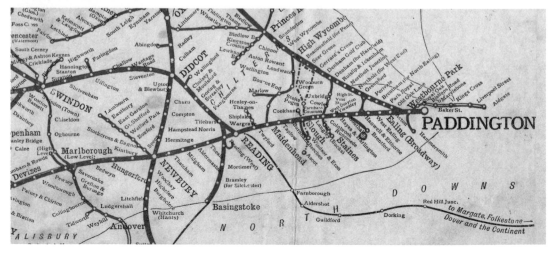

Paddington to Swindon

GREAT WESTERN RAILWAY

London to Slough

The *Metropolitan Terminus* of the Great Western Railway is situated on the western side of the Paddington Canal, in a line with Praed Street, Paddington, at the north-west extremity of London, and at a short distance from the northern avenues to Hyde Park, thus affording an easy access to and from all parts of the town. Omnibuses leave the city one hour before the departure of each train, and call at the booking-offices on their way, which in addition to the cabs, leave the passenger at no loss for a prompt conveyance to this Terminus – one of the largest and most commodious stations in London. Its external appearance is not very remarkable – but the booking-offices are convenient, the waiting-rooms comfortable, the platforms, for the arrival and departure of trains, spacious enough to accommodate the largest number of excursionists ever accumulated – and the vast area embraced by the immense roofs by which the station is covered, impart to the mind of the traveller the impression that he is about to start by the railway of a first-rate company.

It is the joint work of Messers. Brunel and M. D. Wyatt, the former having arranged the general plan, engineering, and business portion; the latter the architectural details in every department. The principle adopted by them, was to avoid any recurrence to existing styles and to make the experiment of designing everything in accordance with the structural purpose or nature of the materials employed – iron and cement. The office buildings are 850 feet long, varying from thirty to forty in width. The departments for directing and managing the affairs of the Company, are carried on in the upper portion of the building, and those in connection with the traffic to and from the station in the lower part.

The space occupied by the platforms and lines of railway under the curved roofing is 700 feet long, and 240 feet 6 inches wide, and contains four platforms and ten lines of railway. The two platforms on the departure side of the station are respectively 27 feet and 24 feet 6 inches wide; and the other two, on the arrival side, are 21 feet and 47 inches. The latter is of stone. The roofing over the above space is divided into three longitudinal openings, with two transepts, each 50 feet wide, at one-third and two-thirds of the length, the length of which are each 700 feet and their respective widths 70 feet, 102 feet 6 inches,

Wharncliffe Viaduct

Striding across the Brent Valley to the west of Hanwell, the 896 foot brick viaduct consists of eight semi-elliptical spans. Originally it was mounted on pairs of elegantly tapered piers, later increased to three when the railway was widened from two tracks of broad gauge to four of the narrower gauge. *Below:* Engraved by J. C. Bourne, the viaduct bears the coat of arms of Lord Wharncliffe who was instrumental in the passing of the act to build the Great Western.

and 68 feet. The central half of the curved roofs is glazed, and the other portion is covered with corrugated galvanized iron. The work was done by Messers. Fox, Henderson, and Co.

On the departure of the train, it threads the sinuosity of the station at an easy rate, and we have time to notice the metamorphosis that has taken place in the environs of the line; walls have become green embankments, embankments diminished into hedges, and hedges grown into avenues of trees, waving a leafy adieu as we are carried past. The increasing velocity of the train now conveys us rapidly into the suburbs of the metropolis – past Kensal Green Cemetery on the right, Wormwood Scrubbs on the left, and a transient glimpse is obtained of the London and North-Western Railway winding its way towards the midland counties.

The route at first lies through the Thames Valley, then, after passing the elevated plains to the north of the Marlborough Downs, it gradually descends down into the fertile and picturesque valley of the Avon. Emerging from a slight excavation, we come to an embankment crossing Old Oak Common so named from it having been the site of a thick forest of oaks. The village of Acton, which lies to the left, is linked to the metropolis by one almost uninterrupted line of houses, through which the North-Western Junction Railway passes, connecting the North-Western Railway with those of the South-Western.

EALING STATION – *Gunnersbury P ark*, Baron Rothschild; *Castlebear Hill*, and *Twyford Abbey*, close by. Thence passing the pretty hamlet of Drayton Green we stop at

HANWELL.
>Distance from station, ¼ mile.
>A telegraph station.
>MONEY ORDER OFFICE at Southall.

From this station the line passes in a gentle curve over the Wharncliffe Viaduct, a massive and elegant structure, which commands extensive views on both sides. The Uxbridge road is seen winding beneath, and afar may be discerned, outlined in the blue distance, the undulating range of Surrey hills, with the rich, leafy, loftiness of Richmond Hill and Park occasionally intervening. In the foreground will be noticed Osterley Park, the seat of the Earl of Jersey; and the most interesting object in the landscape is Hanwell Asylum, generously devoted to the reception of the indigent insane.

SOUTHALL.
>A telegraph station.

Crossing the Uxbridge Road

Left: For the crossing over the awkward intersection on the Uxbridge Road Brunel designed a skew bridge with long iron girders on two rows of masonry pillars. It was badly damaged in 1847 when the wooden decking caught fire.

Slough

Two views of the station at Slough which was one of Brunel's unusual single-sided stations, the other being at Reading. Inevitably this layout with trains crossing over the lines was far from satisfactory and it was later rebuilt.

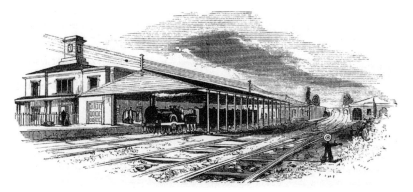

HOTEL – Red Lion.
MARKET DAY – Wednesday.

At this station a short branch 3¾ miles, turns off to the left, by which a connection with the South Western is formed at **Brentford**.

Crossing the Paddington and Grand Junction Canal, we pass alternately through excavation and embankment on to

WEST DRAYTON.

Distance from station, ¼ mile.
A telegraph station.
HOTELS – Crown; King's Head; De Burgh Arms.
MONEY ORDER OFFICE at Uxbridge.

Here, in the early mornings of summer and golden evenings of autumn, descends many a brother of the rod and line, who, in the confluence of the Colne and Crane, finds a prolific source of pleasure from his favourite pastime.

We now cross the western boundary of Middlesex, and then pass over a small corner of Buckinghamshire, between West Drayton and Maidenhead, into the county of Berks.

[UXBRIDGE BRANCH]

Soon after leaving West Drayton we cross the river Colne and its branches, with *Hunt's Moor Park*, and the beautifully sequestered village of Iver (which, alike to artist or antiquary, will be found replete with objects of interest and attraction), on the right, and enter

BUCKINGHAMSHIRE

Arriving at the station at

LANGLEY.
To the right, at a short distance, is Langley Park. A few minutes more brings us to

SLOUGH.

A telegraph station.
HOTEL – Crown.
MARKET DAY – Thursday.

After the bustle incident to the arrival of fresh passengers, and the departures of others, has in some degree subsided, it will be found that

Maidenhead's brick arches

To cross the Thames at Maidenhead, Brunel created a bridge with the two widest and flattest brick-built arches ever seen. With a central pier standing on a shoal mid-stream, the arches each have a span of 128 feet and a rise of just 24 feet 6 inches. The sceptics said it couldn't possibly bear the weight of the railway trains. Clearly they were proved wrong, although Brunel would over-step the mark with another brick bridge at Bridgwater. *See page 54.*

the arrangements for the comfort and convenience of those alighting at this station are equal, if not superior, to those of any other line.

A magnificent hotel, for aristocratic visitors, here so frequently found, is within a few minutes' walk, and numerous taverns, less ornamental, and, consequently, less expensive, are in the immediate neighbourhood.

Slough is now chiefly noticeable as the station or medium of communication, by the branch railway, to Eton and Windsor. It is two and a half miles in length, and passes Eton College, near the Thames.

[WINDSOR BRANCH]

Slough to Maidenhead.

Between the lofty and luxuriant foliage of Stoke Park, about two miles to the right of Slough, may be described, modestly peering through the surrounding trees, the spire of Stoke Pogis Church, the scene of Gray's 'Elergy'. The following inscription to his memory is on the east wall of the church: 'Opposite to this stone, in the same tomb upon which he has so feelingly recorded his grief at the loss of a beloved parent, lie deposited, the remains of Thomas Gray, the author of the 'Elergy written in a Country Churchyard,' &c., &c., etc. He was buried August 6th, 1771.' The church itself has no internal beauty, being over-crowded with pews; but the churchyard is one of the prettiest in England. The cloister is worth a visit. As the train proceeds, the broad and verdant fields spread out on each side of us in all the pride of luxuriant vegetation.

Burnham Village is close by, situated in the midst of picturesque woodland scenery, popularised by the adventures of Albert Smith's Mr. Ledbury.

MAIDENHEAD.

>Population, 3,895.
>Distance from station, 1½ mile.
>A telegraph station.
>HOTELS – White Hart; Bear.
>MARKET DAY – Wednesday.
>FAIRS – Whit Wednesday, September 29th, and November 30th.

[WYCOMBE AND THAME BRANCH]

Sonning Cutting

To the east of Reading the Sonning Cutting slices through the hills. Varying in depth from 20 feet to nearly 60 feet, its excavation was a massive task involving an army of up to 1,200 navvies removing 700,000 cubic yards of material. It was here that Brunel built one of his first timber bridges, *shown above,* to carry a road over the cut.

Left: Sonning Cutting was such a major landmark on the London to Bristol line that the very last broad gauge train to Penzance, the 'Cornishman', paused here for a final photograph in May 1892. However this official photograph appears to show an eastbound train.

Lower left: It is hard to appreciate its scale, but for most of today's high-speed travellers the cutting passes unnoticed in a world of ever bigger civil engineering works.

Maidenhead to Reading

Upon leaving Maidenhead the railway soon spans, by a bridge of ten arches, the river Thames, which here glides through a flat, but most charming country. Having crossed the Windsor road, and diverged gradually to the southward we suddenly dip into an excavation of considerable depth; the characteristic chalky sides of which are replete with geological interest. This cutting, which continues for upwards of five miles, completely shuts out the surrounding country; but coming suddenly upon the Ruscombe embankment, we are amply repaid by a magnificent expanse of landscape. Hill and dale, dotted with elegant villas and noble mansions, woodland and water scenery, together with wide far-stretching meadow and corn-land, follow each other in varied succession to the very verge of the horizon. We have scarcely had time, however, to feast our vision with this delightful prospect, before we are again buried in a cutting, though of shorter duration, and through this we reach the station at

TWYFORD (Junction).
> A telegraph station.
> HOTELS – Station Hotel; King's Arms.

In the neighbourhood are *Stanlake* (1 mile). *Shottesbrooke Church* (2½ miles), a beautiful miniature cross, with a tall tower and spire, formerly attached to an ancient college here. A short line hence branches off to Henley-upon-Thames, passing by *Wargrave*.

> *[HENLEY BRANCH]*

Within a few minutes after quitting the station, we emerge from the excavation, and cross, on an embankment, the river Lodden. From this we enter into another cutting of great depth conducting us to an embankment which affords a pleasing view of the county bordering on the woody lands of Oxfordshire. Crossing, on a level embankment, the river Kennet, we soon after reach the station at

READING.
> A telegraph station.
> HOTEL – Great Western; George; Upper Ship; Angel.
> MARKET DAYS – Wednesday and Saturday.
> FAIRS – Feb. 2nd, May 1st, July 25th, & Sept. 21st.

Reading station
A rare photograph of the single-sided station at Reading. The contemporary engraving of the station interior, *below,* comes from George Measom's *Illustrated Guide to the Great Western Railway* which was first published in 1852. Destined not to outsell Bradshaw's publications, Measom's alternative guide tended to focus much more on the railway itself.

As with Slough the single-sided station at Reading had to be rebuilt. The Reading General Station, as it was known, was built in brick with Bath Stone trimming and opened in 1860. It is shown here a century later in the 1960s. *(Gordon Collier)*

READING is situated on two small eminences, whose gentle declivities fall into a pleasant vale, through which the branches of the Kennet flow till they unite with the Thames at the extremity of the town. The surrounding country is agreeably diversified with an intermixture of hill and dale, wood and water, enlivened with a number of elegant seats. In the Forbury some pleasure grounds have been laid out: a band usually plays there in the summer months. The old abbey ruins have been excavated, and are open to the public. The abbey gateway has also been restored by G. G. Scott Esq., at a cost of £500. Next to it has been built a ponderous County Court at a great expense.

This old town is in a fertile and well-watered part of Berkshire, at the junction of the Thames and Kennet. It returns two members to parliament, and has a population of 25,045. The manor belongs to the corporation. A large and important mitred abbey, founded by Henry I in 1125, to atone for putting out his brother Robert Curthose's eyes frequently attracted the court here down to 1540, when the vigorous defender of the faith, Henry VIII, hung the last abbot for refusing to account for his stewardship. Henry I was buried in it. A Norman gate and part of the outer flint walls (8 feet thick) are left. The latter took in a circuit of half a mile. Reading was inhabited by the Saxons many years before the invasion of the Danes; and it appears that it had two castles, one of which probably stood on the spot where the abbey was founded. In 1263 Henry III held a parliament here, and another was adjourned hither in 1453. Some old gable buildings and ancient looking streets are yet seen at Reading; but a handsome new town has sprung up round Eldon Road and Square, Queen's Road, etc., on the south-east side of the Kennet. St Lawrence's church, near the Forbury, has a chequered flint tower, and remnants of antiquity, with a monument to Dr. Valpy. St Mary's, in St Mary's Butts, was first built in the 12th century, but rebuilt in 1550 with materials from the abbey. Bishop Lloyd was vicar here; as was also the present Dean Millman. There was a nunnery attached to it. St Giles's, in Bridge Street, has been lately restored. It suffered in the long siege of 1642, when Colonel Ashton held the town against Essex. A fine new church has been built at a cost of £7,000, at Whitley, from the designs of Mr. Woodgeare; it is at present the finest church in the town. St James's (Roman Catholic) is one of Pugin's first attempts, and is of the Norman style. It lies at the rear of the site occupied by the old abbey.

The *Town Hall* was built 1785, and contains various portraits, among which are those of Queen Elizabeth, Sir T. White, a native, and the founder of St John's College, Oxford, and that strange compound of intellectual vigour, superstition, and bigoted meanness, Archbishop *Laud*, born at Reading, 1573. He, in common with Merrick, the poet, Addington, the premier, and Lord Chancellor Phipps, all Reading men, was educated in the Grammar School, formerly held beneath the

The Pangbourne-type

Although only a secondary station on the main line, Pangbourne, *above,* was an important one in the Brunel's canon of work as it established a standardised style and design which he used again and again. The original was swept away by the widening of the line, but an identical example has survived at Culham on the quieter Didcot to Oxford line.

Town Hall, originally founded 1486. Laud bequeathed property worth about £500 a year to his native town. Henry VII's charter, with his illuminated portrait, is kept in the Town Hall. A portrait of the late Mr. Justice Talfourd has recently been presented by his widow.

A new cattle market has been built close to the railway station. Great quantities of malt, flour, and timber are sent hence to London. There are a large iron foundry at Ketesgrove, the manufactory for Huntley and Palmer's biscuits, and a model gaol; also several good schools. The old Abbey of the Grey Friars, in Friar Street, formerly used as a borough lock-up, is fast being converted from a den of thieves into a noble church, from designs by Messers. Poulton and Woodman.

Numerous excursions may be made from this town, as there is scarcely a corner of Berkshire which does not deserve a visit; it is full of beech woods, and beautiful country lanes and alleys. The Kennet, Thames, &c., are bordered by luxuriant pasture, and the healthy downs on the west offer a panorama of delightful prospects. To the west of Reading are the Chiltern Hills, which, like the others, are covered with sheep walks. Maiden Early (2 miles) was the seat of Lord Stowell. *Sonning – Holme Park*, the seat of Robt. Palmer, Esq. The walk by the river is beautiful; good fishing and boating. *Sonning* 'Reach' is one of the best courses on the Thames. The church has been restored. *Mapledurham* (M.M. Blount, Esq.) ought to be visited by lovers of the picturesque; there is good fishing. *Bear Wood*, J. Walter, Esq., M.P., the proprietor of the *Times* newspaper. *Billingbear* is the seat of Lord Braybrooke, editor of 'Pepys' Memoirs'. *Wokingham* (6 miles) on the Roman road to Silchester, has an old church, and is within the bounds of Windsor Forest. Towards Windsor is Binfield, and its beech woods, in which Pope used to ramble. Grundy cheese (like Stilton) is made here. At *Silchester*, just over the Hampshire side, are pieces of the walls of a Roman city, the *Calleva Attrebatum. Englefield*, the Saxon *Englafelda*, where the Danes were once defeated, has one of those large parks, so common in Berkshire, and the epitaph by Dryden on the defender of Basing House. On the Oxfordshire side of the Thames are Caversham, W. Crawshay, Esq., which has been rebuilt two or three times since it was visited by Elizabeth and Charles I.

[BASINGSTOKE BRANCH]

Reading to Didcot.

Passing slowly from the station at a pace that affords us a pleasing bird's eye view of the town, we are carried forward on the same level embankment, and crossing the valley of the Thames soon reach the Roebuck excavation. An embankment, followed by a brief though deep cutting, through the grounds of Purley Park, gives us some charming

Through the Thames valley

As the GWR continued on its legendary level course through the Thames Valley – people refer to it as Brunel's billiard table – there are several interesting examples of his work. As the river meanders, the railway crosses by two impressive skew bridges, one at Basildon, *shown above,* and sometimes referred to as the Gatehampton railway bridge, and the other at Moulsford, *left.* They feature intricately curving brickwork and both bridges have been added to as part of the widening of the line.

Lower left: This former station master's house at Steventon is said to have been designed by Brunel and was chosen by the GWR's directors as the midway meeting point between London and Bristol. Because of their obvious usefulness it is not unusual for such buildings to survive long after the stations have gone.

prospects on the Oxfordshire side, with a mass of woodland scenery scattered over the undulating ground, and cresting even the high summits of the Mapledurham hills beyond.

PANGBOURNE.

A telegraph station.

This place is a very ancient one. Roman remains have been discovered. It is connected with *Whitchurch* on the opposite side of the Thames by a wooden bridge, toll one halfpenny.

Soon after leaving the station the railway takes a north-westerly direction, and at the village of *Basildon*, crossing a viaduct over the Thames, leaves behind it the county of Berks, and enters that of Oxford. Pursuing this northerly direction for a short distance, on the borders of the two counties, we pass a deep cutting, whence, crossing on an embankment the river Thames for the last time, we reach the station of

GORING – Here are still visible the remains of a nunnery for Augustines, founded in the reign of Henry II.

WALLINGFORD ROAD station.

WALLINGFORD.

Population, 7,794.
Distance from station, 3 miles.
HOTEL – Lamb.
MARKET DAYS – Tuesday and Friday.
FAIRS – Tuesday before Easter, June 24th, September 29th, and December 17th.

WALLINGFORD, to which the station affords easy access, is an ancient and somewhat picturesque town, agreeably situated on the banks of the venerable Thames, and includes among its 'lions' the remains of a formidable castle. The churches of St Leonard's and St Mary are of great antiquity. St Peter's, a modern edifice, has a tower of very peculiar construction. A massive stone bridge, with nineteen arches, spans the river. It has a considerable trade in corn and malt.

On leaving the station the railway returns into the county of Berks, and the country assumes a more agricultural and less romantic aspect than that which we had previously traversed. Alternately dipping into excavation, and flitting over embankment, we are carried across Hagbourne Marsh, and passing over the Wantage and Wallingford road, we arrive at

DIDCOT (Junction).

A Telegraph station.
MONEY ORDER OFFICE at Wallingford.

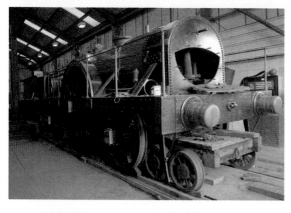

Didcot's trains

Left: The unusual all-over roof design for the large station at Didcot Junction in Oxfordshire. Bradshaw gives us only the basics on Didcot, though George Measom states that it was 'formed on a very large and liberal scale, with every provision for the traffic of an important cross-line'.

Didcot is at the junction between the London to Bristol main line and the branch going up to Oxford and further northwards. Consequently it was developed by the GWR as an important depot and stabling point for the company's steam locos. However, with the end of steam the depot came under the Beeching Axe and it closed in June 1965. Two years later the Great Western Society was offered the site on a lease from British Rail and today it is one of the most important railway heritage attractions in the country. In addition to an impressive gathering of GWR locomotives, large and small, it also has the only working stretch of broad gauge line in the country. This is operated throughout the year by the GWS's *Fire Fly* 0-6-0 working replica, *shown left,* which was completed a year before Brunel's bicentenary in 2006.

Left: Castle-class 5051 was built at Swindon in 1936 as *Drysllwyn Castle,* only to renamed *Earl Bathurst* in the following year. Sent for scrapping in 1963, it was brought to Didcot in 1970. This photograph shows 5051 in steam, but it is currently on static display awaiting a boiler overhaul.

Didcot to Swindon Junction

Leaving Didcot on a rise of seven feet in a mile, we now enter an excavation of about half-a-mile, and emerging thence, bend gradually to the west on an embankment, when again plunging into a short cutting, we are carried past Milton, a small village to the left, and a few minutes afterwards stop at

STEVENTON.

>A telegraph station.
>MONEY ORDER OFFICE at Ablingdon.

Here commences the 'Vale of the White Horse', deriving its singular denomination from the gigantic carving of that useful quadruped, on a high chalky hill beyond – but the cuttings that soon after succeed 'not long, but deep', effectually screen a very pretty country from the eyes of the traveller, save at occasional intervals, when an elevated embankment offers some transient glimpses.

>Borne over the Wiltshire and Berks Canal, we soon after reach
>WANTAGE ROAD for station for

WANTAGE.

>Distance from station, 3½ miles.
>Telegraph station at Faringdon Road, 7¼ miles.
>HOTEL – Bear.
>MARKET DAY – Saturday. FAIRS – First Saturday in March and May, July 18th and October 17th.
>BANKERS – The London and County Bank.

This ancient market town is memorable as the birth-place of our *great* Alfred in 849, and his jubilee in 1849; and during the time of the Saxons it was a royal residence. The famous Wayland Smith's Cave, on Childry Downs, is not far from the town. In the romance of 'Kenilworth', Wayland Smith plays a prominent part, and his character – though founded on a slight foundation – has been drawn by the author of Waverley with amazing power and freshness, forming another of these poetical creations which his wizard pen has left to solace sickness, console sorrow, inspire genius, and defy imitation.

FARINGDON ROAD.

>Distance from the station, 5 miles.
>A telegraph station.
>HOTELS – Bell, Crown.

Broad gauge locomotives

Left: Brunel had many talents, but locomotive design was not one of them. The GWR's first successful locomotive, *North Star,* was purchased from the Stephenson foundry and had originally been intended for an American customer until it was converted to the GWR's broad gauge. It was preserved at the Swindon Works for many years until it was scrapped, only to be rebuilt in replica form, albeit with original driving wheels, in the 1920s. It is now displayed at the Steam museum in Swindon.

Middle: J. C. Bourne's lithograph of *Acheron* emerging from a tunnel. This was one of Daniel Gooch's *Fire Fly* class with a haystack-style firebox.

Lower left: Eponymous replica of the 4-2-2 Iron Duke class loco. The original was built in 1847, and this huge replica currently resides at the Gloucestershire Warwickshire Railway's Toddington station.

MARKET DAY – Tuesday.

FAIRS – February 13th, Whit Tuesday, Tuesdays before and after Michaelmas, and October 29th.

The town is five miles to the right; its church is a very ancient structure, erected on the hill, and contains within several noble monuments; whilst the exterior displays evidence of the havoc committed upon it during the civil wars, the spire having been destroyed by the artillery of the Parliamentary forces. Edward the Elder, one of the Saxon kings, died in a palace here in 925.

To those who duly estimate the worth of a fine prospect, we recommend a visit up the hill to Faringdon High Trees, which, in its extensive survey, includes the major portion of three counties – Oxfordshire, Wiltshire, and Gloucestershire. By sunrise or sunset, a view from this spot is amongst the finest panoramas from nature's exhaustless pencil.

Leaving the station, and progressing on an ascent of about 7 feet in a mile, we are carried on an embankment past the village of Baulking, about two miles distant from which is Kingston Lisle, with its celebrated 'Blowing Stone', in which there are several apertures, and by blowing into any one of these a sound is produced that can be heard for miles distant. Uffington Castle is close by, and a little further on is seen the celebrated *White Horse*, which is carved by order of Alfred, in memory of the triumphant victory, which, in 873, he gained over the Danes, at Ashbury.

SHRIVENHAM.

Distance from station, 1 mile.

A telegraph station.

On leaving this station we pass through an excavation, and thence on an embankment, which commands a fine view of Highworth on the right, and Beacon Hill and Liddington Castle on the summit to the left.

WILTSHIRE

An inland and fertile country, divided into South and North. The aspect of the former displays considerable beauty, as the principal valleys in this division of Wiltshire lie along the banks of the rivers, the most remarkable of which diverge, like irregular radii, from the country around Salisbury and Wilton; these display rich meadows and corn land, interspersed with towns, private residences, and extensive plantations of wood.

North Wiltshire differs completely from the southern division of the county. Instead of the gentle undulations of the south, it appears a complete

The 'Works'

Swindon was chosen by Brunel and Gooch as the GWR's engine works, known more simply by the employees as the 'Works'. The interior of Brunel's engine house is *shown above*; note the traversing trolley to move the locos to and from the side bays.

The company took good care of the army of workers at Swindon. The Railway Village of 300 cottages was devised by Brunel and designed in collaboration with Matthew Digby Wyatt. Constructed between 1841 and 1865, some were built with stone excavated from Box Tunnel.

Bottom left: Swindon's Works in its heyday, the erecting shop photographed in 1927.

level, and is so thickly wooded, that at a short distance it resembles one vast plantation of trees. When examined in detail, however, it is found to contain many fertile and richly cultivated spots. The chief commodities are sheep, wool, wood, and stone, and the principal manufactures are in the different branches of the clothing trade.

SWINDON JUNCTION.

Distance from station, 1 mile.

A telegraph station.

Refreshment rooms at station.

MARKET DAY – Monday.

FAIRS – Monday before April 5th, second Mondays after May 12th and September 11th, second Mondays before October 10th and December 12th.

MAILS – Two arrivals and departures, daily, between London and Swindon.

MONEY ORDER OFFICE.

BANKERS – County of Gloucester Banking Co.; North Wilts Banking Co.

SWINDON, on the Great Western, like Wolverhampton and Crewe on the North Western, is one of the extraordinary products of the railway enterprise of the present age. It is a colony of engineers and handicraft men. The company manufacture their own engines at the factory, where cleaning and everything connected with constructive repair is carried on. The refreshment room at this station is admirably conducted, and abundantly supplied with every article of fare to tempt the best as well as the most delicate appetites, and the prices are moderate, considering the extortions to which travellers are occasionally exposed.

For contractual reasons all trains stopped at Swindon station to enable the long-suffering travellers to experience the infamous refreshment rooms. Bradshaw speaks of them quite favourably, but few others commentators agreed with him.

Wootton Bassett and Chippenham

Beyond Swindon to the west, there is the cutting at Wootton Bassett – the town has become well known in recent years for the scenes of repatriation of fallen servicemen.

Left: This single-storey building beside the station at Chippenham is said to have been used by Brunel as his office during the construction of this part of the line. The station itself is a fine building, although largely obscured by a plethora of later canopies.

Lower left: The entrance into the town itself, through the long railway viaduct, resembles the gateway to some ancient city in this highly romanticised lithograph by Bourne. It is an imposing structure, although he has exaggerated the scale.

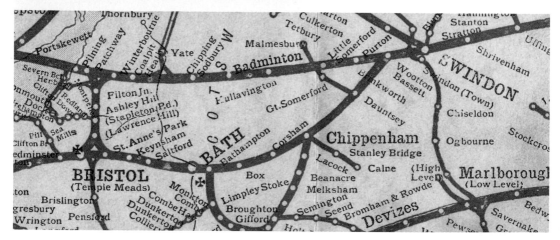

From Swindon to Bristol

GREAT WESTERN RAILWAY

Swindon to Chippenham.

About a mile to the left is the market town [Swindon] which gives its name to the station, and which is now rapidly rising into importance. The old town is pleasantly situated on the summit of a considerable eminence, commanding extensive views of Berkshire and Gloucestershire.

The line here continues on a rapid descent of about 7 feet in a mile, and by embankment crosses several roads, leading from the neighbouring towns and villages. About a mile to the right, is Lydiard, near which can be recognised the lofty trees of the park, the seat of the Bollingbroke family. Sweeping in rather a serpentine course over a richly-cultivated country, we next pass in succession a cluster of small hamlets to our left; and looking forward, scenery of that quiet pastoral description so characteristic of English rural life.

WOOTTON BASSETT.

Distance from station, ¼ mile.
A telegraph station.
HOTEL – Royal Oak.
MARKET DAY – Thursday.
FAIRS – May 4th, Nov 13th, and Dec 19th.

We now proceed on an embankment, having a rapid descent in our favour of about fifty feet in a mile. This elevation affords a comprehensive view of the adjoining valley of 'Bath's Clear Avon' through which the companionable canal is still seen gleaming amid the line of pollards that fringe its edge. Passing through a short excavation we again emerge on a level, whence to the left can be discerned afar off, the stately structure of Bradenstoke Priory. Thence by alternate cutting and embankment we reach

CHIPPENHAM.

POPULATION – 7,075.
Distance from station, ¾ mile.
A telegraph station.
HOTELS – Angel, George.
MARKET DAY – Thursday.

Box Tunnel

Driving 1.83 miles of tunnel through Box Hill was the greatest engineering challenge Brunel faced in constructing the railway. It is also infamous for the heavy toll in human lives with over 100 navvies killed during its construction in the difficult conditions. The tunnel descends on a gradient of 1 in 100 from east to west. In the contemporary illustration, *below,* a signalman is shown to the left of the track at the western portal.

FAIRS – May 17th, June 22nd, Oct 29th, and Dec 11th.
BANKERS – North Wilts Banking Co.; Branch of Wilts and Dorset Banking Co.

This is a parliamentary borough, on the Great Western Railway, in North Wiltshire, on the river Avon, but not otherwise remarkable, except as being a great seat of the cheese trade. Population, 6,283, who send two members to parliament. A little cloth and silk are made. It has two tanneries, a foundry, four banks, a new Town Hall and Market House, built for £12,000 at the cost of J. Neeld, Esq., M.P. of Grittleton, and a long bridge on twenty-three arches. The old church large and handsome. In the time of Alfred it was a city of strength, and was taken by the Danes in 880. It is delightfully situated in a valley on the south bank of the river Avon, by which it is almost surrounded.

In the neighbourhood are *Lacock Abbey*, seat of – Talbot, Esq., the inventor of Photography; *Bowood*, the seat of the Marquis of Lansdowne; *Sloperton*, formerly the seat of Moore, who died in 1852, and is buried at Bromham, near Spye Park, the Starkies' seat. At Bremhill, the poet Bowles died, being the vicar, in 1850.

Calne, a parliamentary borough returning one member, has a large old church. It was here that St Dunstan, then primate, held a synod in 977, to settle a dispute between the clergy and monks, and contrived by making the floor give way, to bring a pretended judgement on his opponents. *Corsham House*, Lord Methuen, is a Tudor building.

Chippenham to Yatton.

Leaving the Chippenham station we continue for some time on an embankment, and then dipping into an excavation we arrive at

CORSHAM.
Distance from station, ¾ mile.
A telegraph station.
HOTEL – Methuen Arms.

King Ethelred had a palace here, and it was once the favourite residence of the Earls of Cornwall. *Corsham House*, the seat of Lord Methuen, has a very fine collection of paintings. Sir Richard Blackmore, the poet, was a native.

Shortly after leaving this station we enter the Box Tunnel which is upwards of one mile and three quarters in length, through the solid heart and immense mass of Box Hill. At intervals a gleam of light appears down the shafts that have been cut through the rock to the surface above. Emerging once more into daylight we proceed over wide-ranging pasture land, spotted with herds and flocks.

Between Box and Bath

Box's other tunnel, the Middle Hill Tunnel, is a little to the west of the village. It has a fine portico, but is much more difficult to access than the Box Tunnel itself which can be viewed from the main road.

Left: More contemporary views by Bourne of the line running through the Avon valley to the east of Bath. The Bathford Bridge over the river and, *below,* the serenity of the countryside right next to the new railway at Bathampton. Bourne saw beauty in both.

Passing Box Station (near which is Wraxhall House), we soon after enter a small tunnel, which is cut through Middle Hill, adjoining a once-noted spa, so called, but now quite forsaken. Emerging from this we pass on an embankment two miles in length that carries the line onward over the Avon into the county of

SOMERSET.

Few of the English counties present so great a variety of scenery and soil as Somerset. It possesses every gradation, from the lofty mountain and barren moor to the rich and cultivated vale, and then descends to the unimprovable marsh and fens. From Taunton to the coast extends a range of hills which slope towards Bridgewater, and on the other side they descend into a cultivated vale. Westward of this, and only terminating in the wild district of Exmoor Forest, the county is entirely mountainous and hilly. Between these there are many steep villages, which form, when richly wooded, some of the most striking features of the beautiful scenery for which this coast is so deservedly celebrated.

Somerset, from its favourable climate and soil, stands very high in reputation for agricultural and rural produce.

The hamlets of Bathford, Bathampton, and Batheaston are now passed in rapid succession, and swerving slightly to the south, the outskirts of the 'Stone-built-city' itself rise in all their magnificence before us, as if evoked by a magician from the fertile pastures we have so recently quitted. A loud and prolonged whistle is borne upon the air as herald of our arrival, and we enter the elegant and commodious station at

BATH.

POPULATION – 52,528.

A telegraph station.

HOTELS – The York House; White Lion; White Hart; The Castle; The Greyhound; Amery's; George's Royal.

OMNIBUSES to and from the station.

MARKET DAYS – Wednesday and Saturday.

BANKERS – Stuckey's Banking Co.; George Moger and Son; Tugwell and Co.; Branch of West of England and South Wales District Bank; National Provincial Bank of England.

The view from the station is one calculated to impress a stranger very favourably with the importance of the city, so renowned in the world of fashionable invalids. He sees on one side of him the river Avon, gliding placidly beneath Pulteney Bridge, and on the other a range of lofty

Sydney Gardens, Bath

The strong curve of the retaining wall and the elegant iron and stone bridges make the cutting through Bath's Sydney Gardens one of the most photographed locations on the whole of the GWR. When built the locals pronounced that the railway had 'been arranged so as to increase, rather than injure, the attractions of the gardens'. But this is a view under threat. Temporary fencing runs beside the low parapet wall and the electrification of the London to Bristol line by 2016 will entail the installation of overhead gantries on this stretch.

hills, studded with terraces and isolated villas, whilst before expand the white edifices of the city. The modern city of Bath is of great beauty, and delightfully situated, in a valley, divided by the river Avon. The surrounding country is well wooded, and, from the inequality of the ground, presents a great variety of beautiful scenery, whilst, from its sheltered position, the temperature of the vale is mild. Lansdowne Hill, nearly three miles in extent, was the scene of a desperate battle, fought there between the royalists and parliamentary forces, terminating in the defeat of the latter. This magnificent elevation is now the most picturesque part of the city, having groves and terraces throned above each other almost to the summit, commanding a prospect of great extent and diversified beauty. Mansions of aristocratic appearance are scattered in all directions; spacious streets, groves and crescents, lined with stately stone edifices, and intersected by squares and gardens, complete a view of city grandeur scarcely surpassed by any other in the kingdom. The gaieties of Bath are celebrated all over Europe; but it must be conceded that, since the reign of Beau Nash, they have terribly degenerated.

Bath is not only renowned for its antiquity and waters, but is one of the best built cities in the United Kingdom, standing in a spot remarkable for its attractive scenery, on the Avon and the Great Western Railway, 107 miles from London, at the centre of a fine circle of hills, 500 to 700 feet high. These hills furnish the blue lias, or oolite, and Bath stone, so much in use by architects, and of which the city has been erected. It is the seat of a bishop, whose diocese extends over Somersetshire, and its population of 54,240 send two members to parliament.

The peculiar virtues of its hot-springs were soon discovered by the Romans, who built a tower here, called *Aquae Solis* (waters of the sun), a name which under the form of Aix, Ax, Aigs, &c., still distinguishes many watering-places on the continent. The Saxons who resorted here significantly styled one of the main roads which led to it, Akeman Strutt, i.e., the road for *aching men*.

Besides the private baths in Stall Street, there are four public ones leased from the corporation. King's Bath, the largest, a space 65 feet by 40, with a temperature of 114°; in the middle of it a statue to 'Bladud, son of Lord Hudibras, eight king of the Britons from Bute, &c., &c., the first discoverer of these baths, 863 years B.C.', and so forth. King's Bath is in Stall Street, on one side of the colonnade and the pump-room, where the band plays. It was rebuilt in 1796, on the site of that in which Beau Nash, with a white hat for his crown, despotically ruled as master of the ceremonies in the last century. His statue is seen here, by Hoare. Over the front is a Greek tee-total motto, signifying 'Water is the thing.' Queen's Bath, close to the other, and so called when James I's queen, Anne of Denmark, came here to take the waters. Hot Bath, which has

Coming into Bath

After straddling the rooftops of Bath on a curving viaduct, the line crosses over the River Avon via the St James's Bridge, an overlooked and very elegant structure, albeit randomly patched up with all manner of brickwork. The station itself is located within an awkward corner on the bend, or elbow, of the river, as shown on the bottom right of the main picture.

10212 - BATH FROM BEECHEN CLIFF

Right: Another depiction of the St James's Bridge, this time seen from the river bank on the north side. Bath's roofed station is shown to the right – *see page 38 for an illustration of the station interior.* Trees and buildings now totally obscure this view of the station.

a temperature of 117° (the highest), and is supplied by a spring which gives out 128 gallons per minute. Cross Bath, temperature 109°, only yielding twelve gallons a minute. This is the one recorded by Pepys in his diary, 1668.

> 'Up at four o'clock, being by appointment called to the Cross Bath. By and by much company came; very fine ladies, and the manners pretty enough, only methinks it cannot be clean to go so many bodies together in the same water. Strange to see how hot the water is;'

and he wonders that those who stay the season are not all parboiled. Another bath is the property of Lord Manvers. The water is nearly transparent; about 180,000 gallons daily are given out to these baths, and this has been going on for centuries! Sulphate of lime is by far the chief ingredient; then muriate and sulphate of soda, and a little carbonic acid rising up in bubbles. They are remarkably beneficial in rheumatism, paralysis, skin complaints, scrofula, gout, indigestion, and chronic diseases of the liver &c. House painters, among others, come here to be cured of the injury done to their hands by white lead.

Bath is a city of terraces and crescents – viz – the Circus, the North and South Parades, the Royal and Lansdowne Crescents, and others, either in the town or on the hills around. Some of the best buildings are by Wood, author of 'Description of Bath.' Among the twenty churches is the Abbey Church, or cathedral, which replaces a monastery, founded in 970, by King Edgar; it is a cross, 240 feet long, built in the sixteenth century, and has fifty-two windows inside, with a rich one in the fine east front, and some good tracery in Prior Bird's Chapel. There are monuments to Waller, the parliament general (effigy, with a broken nose), to Bishop Montague, who restored the church, 1606, to Nash (lines by Dr. Harrington); Quin, the actor (lines by Garrick); Mary Frampton (lines by Dryden); Col. Champion, by Nollekens; and Anstey, author of the coarse witty 'New Bath Guide.'

St James's is a modern Grecian church with a high tower, in Stall Street. Another church, with a fine early English spire, stands in Broad Street. St Saviour's, at the eastern extremity of the city, and St Stephen's, on Lansdowne, are modern Gothic churches; and several others of note. Milson Street and Bond Street contain the best shops. Near are the Circus, and the Assembly Room, a handsome pile, built in 1771 by Wood, with a ball-room 106 feet long, and an octagon full of portraits. Another of Wood's works, the Royal Crescent, is worth notice; Smollett called it 'an antique amphitheatre turned inside out.' The Guildhall, a noble building in the Grecian style, is in High Street. Near at hand is a well-stocked market. Its supply of fish is very good.

Within a short distance is the General Hospital, founded chiefly through Beau Nash's exertions, for the benefit of poor people, from all

Bath station

This is something of an oddity. The interior view of Bath station with its all-over wooden roof, now long gone, bears more than a passing resemblance to the images of Temple Meads in Bristol – *see page 42.* But for the exterior of this station building located in a town widely celebrated for its fine Georgian architecture, Brunel chose an Elizabethan country house style. Upon entering the building you discover stairs that lead upwards to the line and platforms which are on the upper level or storey.

Lower left: Exiting westwards from the station the rails immediately cross the Avon again, this time on a sharp skew. This is Brunel's wooden bridge which has since been replaced by a steel latticework bridge. Beyond the river the railway continues on another long viaduct, hugging the A4 road until it enters the tunnel and cuttings at Twerton.

parts, using the Bath waters. Bellot's Hospital, an old building, founded in 1609. The Casualty and United Hospitals are among the various munificent institutions here. Partis's College was founded for ladies of decayed fortune. St John's Hospital, founded in the 12th century, and rebuilt by Wood, near Cross Bath, has an income of £9,000.

There is a full and interesting museum of Roman antiquities and fossil remains at the Literary Institution, near the Baths and Parade. A club-house in York Buildings, and several public libraries.

A large Grammar School, rebuilt in 1752, stands in Broad Street; here Sir Sidney Smith was educated. Beau Nash died in St John's Court, 1761, old and neglected. A well-built theatre is in Beaufort Square. The Sydney or Vauxhall Gardens at Great Pulteney Street (so called after the Pulteney who became the first Earl of Bath). Victoria Park, with a drive, pillar, botanic garden, &c., occupies the Town Common. There are also obelisks to the Prince of Orange and the Prince of Wales, father of George III. The new savings bank, in the Italian style, was built in 1842.

Of the nine bridges over the Avon there are suspension bridges, two are viaducts for the railway, and the best looking is that on the North Parade, a single arch of 188 feet span.

All the hills command fine views, of more or less extent, and are marked by buildings, &c. On Odd Down (south) is the Union Workhouse. A vast quarry of Bath stone is opened in Coomb Down (south west), on which are the Abbey Church Cemetery, and Prior Park College – a handsome building. In Pope's time it was the property of his friend, Ralph Allen (the Allworthy of Fielding's *Tom Jones*), and Warburton. Allen built Sham Castle, on Claverton Down. The beautiful vale of Lyncombe is near this. Lansdowne Hill, 813 feet high, on the north has a cemetery, two large colleges, one belonging to the Wesleyans; pillar to the memory of Sir B. Granville, who fell here in 1645, and a striking campanile tower built by Beckford of Fonthill, who died here in 1844, and is buried in the cemetery. He wrote 'Caliph Vathek', a most original story, which created quite a *'furore'* in those days. His daughter, the beautiful Sally Beckford, is Dowager Duchess of Hamilton.

Other points are Batheaston Church and Salisbury Hill, 600 feet high, near the old Roman road, on the east; Hampton Cliffs at Bathford, on the west; Charlecombe and Weston Downs; Kelston (or Kelweston) Round. At Twerton a factory for the cloth or Bath coating for which the town was once noted. Paper is made here. Further off are the ruins of Hinton Priory and Farleigh Castle.

The 'ever-memorable' John Hales, and Miss Edgeworth's father (whose entertaining memoirs are well worth perusal), were born at Bath.

From the Bath station the railway is carried on a viaduct, continued by alternate excavation and embankment, over the Old Bath Road. We

The Avon Valley from Bath to Bristol

The section of line winding beside the Avon along the valley from Bath to Bristol is not necessarily the most accessible or, for that matter, the most photogenic part of the railway nowadays. But this was not always the case and Brunel originally imbued what was a very picturesque stretch of line with a number of gems.

Top left: The Gothic portal of the tunnel at Saltford. Admittedly the tunnel doesn't look that impressive when viewed through a telescopic lens, however it is over 500 feet long and, as you can see, passes directly under this house. Best seen from the footbridge to the east, but you might need to take some steps to stand on.

Left: Brunel turned a rockfall to good advantage in creating this fashionably ruinous entrance to 'Tunnel No.2' near Bristol.

Last two images: A distant view of the Bristol with its tall factory chimneys belching smoke, *c.* 1846. Seen from the south-east of the city with the railway bridge passing over the Avon on the right-hand side on its way into Temple Meads. This fine masonry bridge is still there, but it has been almost totally hidden behind later steel structures added on either side.

soon after pass into an excavation and then through a tunnel. Amid a succession of very varied and beautiful scenery along the line, we reach the station of

      TWERTON, and soon after, that of

SALTFORD.

      Telegraph station at Keynsham, 2½ miles.
      HOTEL – Railway.

A very deep excavation here follows, and through a Gothic gateway conducts us to the Saltford Tunnel. An embankment succeeds across the valley of the Avon, and passing over a viaduct we arrive at

KEYNSHAM.

      Distance from station, ¼ mile.
      A telegraph station.
      HOTEL – White Hart.
      MARKET DAY – Thursday.
      FAIRS – March 24th and 26th, April 27th, and August 15th.

Proceeding over a lofty embankment, which affords a commanding prospect on every side, and enables us to trace the windings of the silvery Avon, along its verdant shores, edged with towering poplars and branching elms. Nature here seems to have put on her loveliest robe, but Art, as if envious of her beauty, jealously encloses us in a ponderous cutting at the very moment we are most enthusiastically enjoying the prospect.

    The train passes through several tunnels, and flitting over a three-arched bridge that spans the Avon, we again reach an embankment, during our passage over which our speed is gradually slackened, and we pass beneath that splendid archway, the entrance to

BRISTOL.

      POPULATION – 154,093.
      Distance from station, 1 mile.
      A telegraph station.
      HOTELS – The Queen's Hotel; Clifton.
      OMNIBUSES to and from the station.
      MARKET DAYS – Wednesday, Friday, and Saturday.
      FAIRS – March 1st and September 1st.
      BANKERS – Branch of the Bank of England; Ballie, Ames, and Co.; Miles and Co.; Stuckey's Banking Co.; National Provincial Bank of England; West of England and South Wales District Banking Co.

Temple Meads, Bristol

The world's first purpose-built railway terminus. The facade repeats the mock-Elizabethan styling. The building served as offices and as the meeting room for the Bristol board of the GWR. The entrance was through the arch on the left, and carriages would pass underneath the track to emerge on the right-hand side and exit through a corresponding arch.

Left: The interior of the passenger shed, with the engine shed beyond. The hammerhead detail on the wooden beams is purely decorative. Note the carriages mounted on the flat-bed railway trucks.

Bottom left: The wooden goods shed was an equally interesting building, although much plainer and simple in comparison with the station. Brunel's station has survived virtually intact, but the goods shed has gone.

The terminus is situated on an eminence rising from Temple Meads, where the two lines diverge respectively to London and Plymouth.

BRISTOL is a cathedral city, sea-port, and parliamentary borough in Gloucestershire, 118 miles from London, on the Great Western Railway, and the *Via Julia*, or Roman road, made by Julius Agricola, which crossed into Wales at Aust Ferry. The beautiful watering place of *Clifton* is on the west side. *Bedminster*, within the borough bounds, belongs to Somerset. Its port is artificially made by excavating floating docks, three miles long, out of the old bed of the Avon (for which a new course was made), about eight miles from King's Road in the Bristol Channel, the tide rising 40 to 50 feet. Since the tolls were reduced in 1848, the registered tonnage has risen to 71,000 and the foreign trade doubled. Much West India and Irish produce finds its way into the country through this port. The chief manufactures are engines, glass, hats, pottery, soap, brushes &c., besides various smaller branches, and a trade in sugar, rum &c. this place has, from the earliest times, been an important seaport, from whence old navigators used to start. One of the foremost was Sebastian Cabot, a native, who sailed hence in 1497 to discover Labrador. Kidnapping, also, for the American plantations used to be practised here, and it shared with Liverpool the iniquities of the slave trade. In the present day it is noted for having sent the first steamer across the Atlantic, the *Great Western* (Capt. Hosken), which sailed on the 2nd May 1838, and reached New York in fifteen days. Two members. Coal and oolite are quarried.

The oldest part of the town is in Temple, Peter, and other streets, where picturesque timber houses are seen. There are many buildings worth notice. At College Green (where a new High Cross has been erected) is the Cathedral, a plain, shapeless, early English church, built in 1142-60, and about 174 feet long internally; it has a tower 133 feet high, with some effigies of the Berkeleys, &c., and various interesting monuments and inscriptions. The latest is that of Southey, a native. Near is a Norman chapter-house 43 feet long, the cloisters, gate, &c., of a priory house founded by the Berkeley family; also a part of the Bishop's Palace, set fire to in the riots of 1831, when Wetherall was appointed Recorder. The bishop now resides at Stapleton. A more interesting church is that of *St Mary Redcliffe*, a truly beautiful early and later English cross, 247 feet long, rebuilt in the fifteenth century by the famous William Canynges, and now partly restored. St John's, St Peter's, St Stephen's, St James's, the Temple and St Mark's are all ancient edifices. At All Saints, E. Colston, a great benefactor to his native place, is buried. The *Guildhall*, in Broad Street, has been rebuilt in the Elizabethan style, and among other curiosities it contains an ancient chapel. Henry VII's sword (he visited in 1487, taking care to entail a sumptuary fine on the citizens because their wives dressed too gaudily), a series of grants from 1164, seals from Edward I, Lord

Clifton

Another Brunel landmark in Bristol. As Bradshaw comments the bridge was not finished by the time the guide was published. It was only completed after IKB's death and in its final form it varies in many details from Brunel's design. New lighting was installed in 2006.

Bradshaw also mentions the Observatory at Clifton. A former snuff mill it was partially destroyed by fire before conversion as a camera obscura. A convex lens and sloping mirror mounted at the top of the tower, project a panoramic view onto a table in a darkened chamber. The result is a true and moving image of the surroundings.

Wallis's pearl scabbard sword (given in 1431), and Alderman Kitchen's silver salver (as old as 1594), which, being stolen in the riots of 1831, was cut into 167 pieces, *recovered, and put together again!*

Other buildings are, the Council House, with a statue of Justice, by *Baily* (who is a native); new Custom-house (rebuilt since the riots, in Queen Square, near William of Orange's statue; Exchange, in Corn Street, built by Wood of Bath, in 1743, Merchant Tailors' Old Hall, in Broad Street; Stuckey's Bank, which was sent ready made from Holland; Philosophical Institution, with Baily's exquisite *Eve at the Fountain* in the museum. Bishop's College and the Blind asylum are in the Park, near the Horticultural Rooms; Proprietary and Baptist Colleges; Queen Elizabeth's Hospital on Brandon Hill, which is 250 feet high.

St Vincent's Rocks are 300 feet high; at the Observatory a suspension bridge over the Avon to Leigh Wood is begun, but not finished. Another beautiful spot is at the Zoological Gardens, near Cook's Folly, on Durdham Down. The *Clifton Hot Wells,* or sulphur springs, near here, are excellent in cases of scrofula and chronic diseases. The following most feeling lines were written at this place by the second Lord Palmerston, in the last century:

> 'Whoe'er, like me, with trembling anguish brings
> His dearest earthly treasure to these springs,
> Whoe'er, like me, to soothe distress and pain,
> Shall court the salutary springs in vain;
> Condemn'd, like me, to hear the faint reply,
> To mark the fading cheek, the sinking eye;
> From the chill brow to wipe the damps of death,
> And watch in dumb despair the shortening breath,
> If chance should bring him to this humble line
> Let the sad mourner know this pang was mine,
> Ordained to love the partner of my breast,
> Whose virtue warmed me, and whose beauty blessed;
> Framed every tie that binds the heart to prove,
> Her duty friendship, and her friendship love;
> But you remembering that the parting sigh
> Appoints the just to slumber, not to die,
> The starting tear I checked – I kissed the rod,
> And not to earth resigned her – but to God.'

Lansdowne Square, Windsor and York Crescents, and the Victoria Rooms (a pretty Grecian temple), are here. On the Down above, there is a Roman camp. Here many plants, and quartz or Bristol stones are found. Mr. Pepys records his approval of another native production, 'Bristol milk, or old sherry', At Temple Mead are various metal works, sugar refineries, &c. One of Wesley's first chapels was built in 1739 in the Horse Fair; and there is a Wesleyan College at Kingswood (four miles off) where Whitfield and he often preached the Gospel to the poor outcast colliers, till the 'tears made white gutters down their black cheeks.'

Admiral Penn, Sir Thomas Lawrence (born at the White Lion), and Chatterton, are among the long list of natives of Bristol.

Twelve or more bridges cross the Avon and the line of Docks – the cutting forming a sort of loop line to the river. Of about 120 places of worship, forty-two are churches.

Within a short distance are *Leigh Court* and its picture gallery, the seat of P. Miles, Esq., M.P. Kingsweston, the Clifford's old seat, belongs to the same gentleman. *Stapleton* is the seat of the Bishop of Gloucester and Bristol, near the new diocesan college; Hannah More was born here in 1744, but her chief residence was at Barley Wood, under the Mendip Hill. At *Westbury*, 'in some of the finest ground in that truly beautiful part of England', Southey was living about 1796 or 1797, writing *Madoc* and *Thalaba*, and cultivating his acquaintance with Davy, the chemist, 'a miraculous young man'. This was one of the 'happiest portions' of his useful and contented literary life. The rail should be followed to Clevedon or Weston-super-Mare, to enjoy the fine coast scenery of the Bristol Channel.

CLIFTON, a beautiful suburb of Bristol, from which it is about a mile distant, is chiefly built on the southern acclivity of a steep hill or cliff, which has given rise to its appellation. The highly romantic and picturesque country, in the midst of which it is situated, provides on every side the most varied and extensive prospects. On the opposite shore of the Avon, the richly cultivated lands of Somerset present themselves, rising gradually from the verge of the river to the summit of Dundry Hill. In some places the rocks, venerably majestic, rise perpendicularly, or overhanging precipices, craggy and bare, and in others they are crowned with verdure of the most luxuriant description. The walks and rides are varied and interesting, the air is dry and bracing, and the vicinity of two such animated places as Bristol and Bath, give the resident at any time the opportunity of rapidly exchanging his solitude for society. The 'Hot Wells', where 'pale-eyed suppliants drink, and soon flies pain', are beautifully situated beneath the rocks looking on the river, along the banks of which a fine carriage-road leads from the well round the rocks to Clifton Down, but a readier and more picturesque mode of access is furnished by an easy serpentine path winding up among the cliffs behind the Hot Wells. Pieces of the rock, when broken, have much the appearance of a dark red marble, and when struck by a substance of corresponding hardness, emit a strong sulphurous smell. In the fissures of these rocks are found those fine crystals, usually called Bristol diamonds, which are so hard as to cut glass and sustain the action of fire. The spring has been known for many centuries, but it was not till 1690 that it was enclosed by the corporation of Bristol. There is now a neat pump-room with hot and cold baths. The temperature of the spring, which yields forty gallons a minute is 76° Fahrenheit. As at Bath and Buxton, the predominating constituents are the salts of lime. When drawn into a glass the water emits few bubbles of carbonic and gas, and for various conditions of deranged health it is found to be a potent restorative. The range of buildings called York Crescent, affords an agreeable southern aspect, but the elevated situation leaves the houses much exposed to high winds. The Mall, the Parade, and Cornwallis Crescent furnish excellent accommodation to visitors, and according to their respective differences of position, yield a sheltered winter or an open airy summer residence. The most prevalent winds are those from the west and south-east. Rain frequently falls, but from the absorbent nature of the soil, the ground quickly dries. The Giant's Cave is contained within the upper beds of the limestone in St Vincent's Rocks. The cavern opens on the precipitous escarpment of the rock, at the height of about 250 feet above the river, and 60 feet below or to the west of the Observatory. A rude and broken ledge extends from the north-eastern summit of the rock downwards to within twenty feet of the opening, across which space none but an expert cragsman would venture to pass. The environs of Clifton are replete with scenery of the most enchanting description.

This curved section beside the main road is all that remains of the Clifton Hot Wells. Bradshaw proclaimed the sulphurous spring water to be 'excellent in cases of scrofula and chronic diseases'.

The Bristol & Exeter Railway

Bristol's Temple Meads was home to more than one railway station. The Bristol & Exeter Railway, with Brunel as engineer, had a station at right angles to the GWR's. The B&ER office building was built in 1854 to a design by architect Samuel Fripp – not Brunel this time – in a Jacobean style. The broad gauge line to Exeter was completed in 1844 and the company was amalgamated with the GWR in 1876.

The Bristol to Exeter

BRISTOL AND EXETER RAILWAY

Bristol to Hanwell

On leaving the station at Bristol, the lofty roof and portly walls glide away almost insensibly from our vision, and leave us in exchange the free air and undulating grounds of a wide and open country, through which the continuous iron line is seen wending onward. The embankment on which we are carried reveals to us passing glimpses of luxuriant lands, and tower-crested eminences, fertile to the summit, the chief charms and characteristics of all Somerset. About two miles from Bristol we pass under the old turn pike road to Wells and Bridgwater, and in another mile come upon an elevation which unfolds a bold and romantic view of the surrounding country. Ashton Hill, and Leigh Down, with the pretty picturesque village of Long Ashton, form a very attractive picture to the right; and opposite, soaring above the level of the sea to 700 feet, rises the majestic eminence of Dundry Beacon, the turreted summit of which becomes a prominent object for many miles. A cutting here intercepts the view and we pass the stations of

BOURTON, NAILSEA and YATTON, places of no importance, except the latter as being the junction of the
CLEVEDON BRANCH.

After leaving Yatton we catch a very pleasing View of the [Bristol] Channel, with its dimpled surface spotted with white sails, and its range of ruddy headlands stretching far away in the distance. Green hills, diversified by open downs and richly cultivated corn lands, constitute a delightful contrast in the opposite direction; and thus, amid a varied succession of prospects, we reach the station at

BANWELL.
        Distance from station, 2¼ miles.
        Telegraph station at Yatton, 3½ miles.

This little village has become of some notoriety from the discovery of two caverns in the vicinity, one called the Stalactite, and the other the Bone Cave, which attracts a great number of visitors. Locking and Hatton adjacent, with their antiquated churches – the cavern of Wokey,

Flax Bourton

Left: One of the smaller stations on the former Bristol & Exeter Railway, it opened in June 1860 as Bourton – the Flax being added later – and was closed by Beeching in 1964. These derelict buildings date from 1893 when a new station was constructed to the west of the original one.

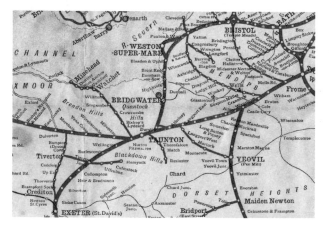

Bridgwater

Built to a design by Brunel, the whitish paintwork, canopies and flat roof give Bridgwater's station the air of a seaside building. It opened in June 1841 and for the first year it served as the southernmost terminus for the Bristol & Exeter Railway until the Black Bridge over the River Parrett was completed – *see page 54.*

and the Cheese-celebrated cliffs of Cheddar, are all worth visiting.

Leaving the Banwell station, we pass the villages of Wick, St Lawrence, Kewstoke, and further on, Worle Hill, which commands a series of extensive maritime and inland views, and variegated landscapes.

[WESTON-SUPER-MARE Junction.]

HIGHBRIDGE.

> Distance from station, ½ mile.
> A telegraph station.
> HOTEL – Railway.
> MONEY ORDER OFFICE at Burnham.

The scenery around here exquisitely pastoral, and almost immediately after quitting the station, the majestic hill known as Glastonbury Tor is seen in the distance, and can be distinctly discerned, with its ruined temple on the summit, though thirteen miles off. The neighbourhood abounds with religious monuments.

[BURNHAM (Branch)]

BRIDGWATER.

> Distance from station, ¼ mile.
> A telegraph station.
> HOTELS – Royal Clarence, Globe, White Hart.
> MARKET DAYS – Tuesday, Thursday, and Saturday.
> FAIRS – Second Thursday in Lent, June 24th, Oct 2nd.

A port and borough in Somersetshire, on the Great Western Railway, twenty-nine miles from Bristol, a bay, and the mouth of the Parrett. Common red bricks of an excellent quality, and the white scouring 'Bath Brick' as it is called, though peculiar to Bridgwater, is only made here by two or three firms. They are manufactured from the slime deposited on the banks of the Parrett, where untouched by the salt water (which spoils it), and burnt at the top of the kiln, above the red bricks.

It returns two members, and has a population of 11,320. About 8,500 tons of shipping belong to the port; small vessels of 200 tons come up to the quay. Admiral Blake was born here in 1599, the son of a merchant. He sat for his native town in parliament. 'He was the first man (says Clarendon) who brought ships to contemn castles on shore, which ... were discovered by him to make a noise only; and ... who infused that proportion of courage into the seamen, by making them see what mighty things they could do if they were resolved.' There was a fortress on Castle Hill, built after the Conquest, by Walter de Douai, from whom, or from the bridge which he began, the town takes its name, Bridge-Walter.

At this spot the Duke of Monmouth was proclaimed, before the defeat at *Sedgemoor*, 1685. It is a level marshy tract, four miles south east, intersected by the Cary, but much altered since that event. Many of the wretched prisoners were brought here to be butchered by Jefferies and his satellite, Kirke.

The large Gothic parish church has a good porch, and a fine spire, 174 feet high, with the 'Descent from the Cross', after Guido. Other buildings are the Town Hall, with a great cistern over it, for supplying the town with water, a Market House, surmounted by a dome, &c., but none very remarkable.

In the neighbourhood are *Brymore House*, seat of Hon. P. Bouverie, where Payne, 'King Payne', of the Long Parliament, lived. *Enmore Castle*, Earl Egmont, *Halsewell*, Colonel Tynte; gallery of Vandykes, &c. All these are to the west of the town, in view of the Quantock Hills; and the road may be followed to Watchet, Dunster, Minehead, and other rocky parts of the coast. At Nether Stowey, Coleridge lived, in 1796-8, after his marriage, in company with his friend Charles Lloyd, the poet; and here he wrote his 'Ancient Mariner', and the tragedy of 'Remorse'. Wordsworth at the same time was his neighbour, at Alfoxton or Allfoxden, where he composed his 'Lyrical Ballads', the subject of many interminable discussions with the friends, as they walked over the hills together.

DURSTON JUNCTION.

Durston to Tiverton and Exeter

On leaving the Bridgwater station the line is continued by embankment across the river Parrett, and soon after we enter the fertile valley of the Tone. The river, which gives name to this luxuriant district rises in the Quantock hills, near the town of Wivelscombe, and, flowing for some miles, passes Taunton, to which town it gives name. Taunton Dean is famed for its fruitful ground, which is proverbially alleged to produce three crops a year. After gliding along several scenes of wild fertility and romantic beauty, we pass a hill which quite shuts out the prospect, and entering a brief but deep cutting, we reach the neat and commodious station at

TAUNTON.

  A telegraph station.
  HOTELS – Castle; London Inn.
  MARKET DAYS – Wednesday and Saturday.
  FAIRS – June 17th and July 7th.

The town, as seen from the station, has a most pleasing appearance. It is situated in the central part of the luxuriant and beautiful vale of Taunton Dean.

TAUNTON is an ancient borough town, population 14,667 (two members), in a rich and beautiful part of Somersetshire, on the Bristol and Exeter Railway, 163 miles from London. The wide and cultivated dean, or shallow strath, in which it stands is watered by the Tone (wherefore the Saxons called it Tantun), and overlooked by the tower of its Gothic church, which is of Henry Seventh's age. The tower is 153 feet high, of light and elegant proportions, covered over with heads of lions, &c., and set off with pinnacles, battlements and niches, in the elaborate style of that day of which, indeed, Somersetshire furnishes many excellent specimens. There is some good carved work inside, about the pulpit and niches, and a fine organ. Quaint epitaph to Sheriff Grey, founder of a hospital, who left this place a poor boy:

'Taunton bore him – London bred him,
Piety trained him, virtue led him,
Earth enriched him, Heaven caressed him,
Taunton blest him, London blest him;
This thankful town, that mindful city,
Shared his plenty and his pity;
What he gave and how he gave it
Ask the poor, and you shall have it,
Gentle reader, may Heaven strike
Thy tender heart to do the like;
And now thy eyes have read this story,
Give him the praise, and Heaven the glory.'

And another on a tailor, who invented ruffs. The *Assize Court* is an ancient building, 120 feet long, erected in 1577, close to the gate of the Castle, which was founded here by Ina, King of Wessex, and rebuilt after the Conquest by the Bishops of Winchester. It was successfully defended by Blake against the Royalists in the civil war, but dismantled by Charles II. Here the ill-fated Monmouth proclaimed himself king in 1685. Forty young ladies presented him with a banner, worked at the cost of the town, for which they were specially expected in King James' proclamation of amnesty, issued some months afterwards. After his defeat at Sedgemoor, near Bridgwater, King James's Chief Justice, Jefferies, the worthy tool of such a monster, held his bloody assize at Taunton, when *hundreds* of poor wretches were condemned to death, after being persuaded to throw themselves on the king's mercy. His executioner, Kirke, hanged one man three times on the White Hart sign post, and cried out he would do it again if he could. The joy of the town therefore, when the Prince of Orange appeared,

Bridgwater station and the Black Bridge over the River Parrett
The station at Bridgewater seen from the south footbridge, looking north. *Below:* To cross the navigable River Parrett to the south of Bridgwater, Brunel constructed a brick span 100 foot wide and even flatter than those at Maidenhead. Work started in 1838 but settlement of the foundations meant that the bridge had to be torn down and replaced by a wooden structure. The present steel girder bridge dates from 1904, and only the lower masonry arches have survived from Brunel's ill-fated bridge.

was proportionally great. The Town Hall and Assembly Room, built in 1723, are over the market place, which stands in an open spot at the junction of the principal streets, called the Parade. A new room at the Taunton Institution was established in 1823. There is now being built a new Shire Hall, to be used instead of the old assize courts. The streets are in general airy and well built, which adds considerably to the pleasant aspect of the town. The outskirts are furnished with large spreading gardens and orchards. One of the best and most conspicuous buildings is the *Wesleyan Collegiate Institution*, a Tudor range, 250 feet long (built 1847); it contains room for 100 students. This, among others, was the result of the centenary celebration.

A little outside Taunton, across the Tone, is Price's Farm, the site of a friary; and in this direction you come on a very ancient bridge, of one arch, called Ram's Horn, and which is said to be a Roman structure.

Within a short distance of Taunton are also *Pyrland*, the seat of R. King Esq. Sandhill, that of Sir T. Lethbridge, Bart., is near Combe Florey, the rectory formerly of Sydney Smith. *Milverton*, in a pretty spot, was the birth place of the philosopher, the late Dr. Thomas Young. *Ninehead* is the seat of E. Sandford, Esq.

The West Somerset, a line of fourteen miles long, turns off here to the right and runs through BISHOPS LYDEARD, CHAWCOMBE, STOGUMBER, and WILLITON, to the market town of
WATCHET.

Leaving the Taunton station we are subjected for a short time to the confinement of a cutting, on passing which we perceive the Bridgwater and Taunton canal on our left, while the eminences to our right are crowned with picturesque villages. Proceeding on an embankment, the little hamlet of Bishop's Hall is passed, and we soon after cross several streams tributary to the Tone, that gleam and sparkle between the patches of meadow land and their forest scenery by which we are skirted in their progress. After crossing a viaduct over the Tone, the arch of Shaw bridge, and passing an excavation, we are carried forward by a sinuous embankment to

WELLINGTON.
> POPULATION 3,689.
> A telegraph station.
> Distance from the station, ½ mile.
> HOTEL – Squirrel.
> MARKET DAY – Thursday.
> FAIRS – Thursday before Whit Sunday, Easter and Holy Thursday.

Taunton

The old station forecourt at Taunton, opened in July 1842 on the Bristol & Exeter Railway. This elegant building dates from 1868 when Brunel's original single-sided station was upgraded. A new ticket hall was added on the northern side of the line in the 1990s.

Left: The water tower at Taunton, a reminder of the town's railway heritage.

Below: 1890, a scene of carnage at Norton Fitzwarren when a standard gauge goods loco collided head-on with a broad gauge express. Ten passengers were killed and many more were injured.

Here is a Gothic church of which W. S. Salkeld was rector in James I's time. The Duke of Wellington, who derives his title from this place, is lord of the manor. A pillar, in honour of the Hero of Waterloo, was erected on Blackdown Hill. This range of hills is on the Devonshire borders, and produces stone used by scythe grinders, &c.

Quitting the station, and again crossing the Tone, we enter an excavation which conducts us to the White Ball Tunnel, a fine piece of arched black brick work nearly one mile in length. About the centre we attain the highest elevation between Bristol and Exeter, and on emerging from its obscuration we find ourselves in the magnificent county of Devon, with the Wellington memorial cresting the summit of a distant hill on our left, and the long range of precipices, known as the Blackdown Hills, far away before us, apparently extending to the very verge of the sea.

DEVONSHIRE

THIS county is one of the most beautiful in England, and in point of size is only exceeded by that of York. It is about 280 miles in circuit. Its external appearance is varied and irregular; and the heights in many parts, particularly in the vicinity of Dartmouth, swell into mountains.

Dartmoor, and the waste called Dartmoor Forest, occupy the greater portion of the western district, which extends from the vale of Exeter to the banks of the river Tamar.

The cultivated lands of West Devon are nearly all enclosures, being in general large in proportion to the size of the farms. North Devon comprehends the country around Bideford.

Amidst a succession of scenery almost purely pastoral we are again startled by the premonitory whistle of the engine, and find ourselves opposite
TIVERTON JUNCTION (Uffculme).

Leaving the Tiverton junction, the line is continued for some time on an embankment, but the beauty of Devonshire scenery is more to be found in the village lanes and unfrequented byways, than near the somewhat mountainous levels which a railway of necessity maintains. Thus the six miles' walk across the hills from Tiverton to Collumpton is a marvellous treat to the pedestrian, whereas the railway tourist sees nothing but a rather dreary succession of green flats, this particular part being devoid of those striking characteristics in the landscape we have hitherto described, and the view of which renders the journey so interesting.

Wellington and the White Ball Tunnel

Left: Two photographs of the goods shed at Wellington. While many station buildings have been lost over the years, goods sheds such as this example survived because they could be easily adapted for other uses, mostly commercial.

Below: Continuing southwards the trains had to tackle steep gradients, averaging 1 in 80, on the Wellington Bank up into the Blackdown Hills, the highest obstruction on the line to Exeter, before passing via a tunnel through White Ball Hill. Started in 1842 this 3,270 foot-long tunnel was excavated by 1,000 navvies and was completed two years later.

COLLUMPTON.

Distance from the station, ¼ mile.

A telegraph station.

HOTEL – White Hart.

MARKET DAY – Saturday.

FAIRS – May 12th and October 28th.

BANKERS – Branch of Devon Banking Co.

This little town, though containing a population of only 3,185, is one of great antiquity, having been in the possession of Alfred the Great, and afterwards belonging to Buckland Abbey. It has some manufactories for woollen and paper.

HELE.

A telegraph station.

MONEY ORDER OFFICE at Collumpton.

Again borne onwards by our never-tiring iron steed, at a speed outstripping the breeze of summer, we become conscious of a moving panorama, which has regained most of the alluring features that we have been recently regretting.

We traverse the valley of the Culme – past Brabninch, through cutting and over embankment – and the winding Exe and Cowley Bridge, and then, after a few minutes of woodland scenery, our speed slackens, the well-known whistle of the engine follows, and we are hurried beneath the portico of a commodious building, which forms the station at

EXETER.

A telegraph station.

FLY FARES – To and from any part of the City, 1s; to and from Heavitree, 1s 6d; to and from Mount Radford, 1s 6d; beyond the boundaries of the City, 1s per mile. A fraction of a mile considered as a mile.

MARKET DAYS – Tuesday and Friday.

FAIRS – Ash Wednesday, Whit-Monday, August 1st, and Dec 6th.

BANKERS – Milford and Co.; Sanders and Co.; Branch of West of England and South Wales District Bank; Branch of Devon and Cornwall Banking Co.; National Provincial Bank of England.

EXETER is pleasantly situated on an eminence rising from the eastern bank of the river Exe, which encompasses its south-west side, and over which it has a handsome stone bridge.

Exeter is the capital of Devon and the West of England, a Bishop's see, city, and parliamentary borough, on the Great Western (Bristol and Exeter) Railway, 194 miles from London. It is also a port, eight miles from the Channel, up the Exe, from which it derives the Saxon name, Excester, or the fortress on the Exe, so called because of the Roman station planted here. Population, 41,749; two members. Exeter stretches for nearly two miles over a hill above the river, and is, therefore, not only pleasantly seated, but well drained, except in some parts of the suburbs. At the top, north of the town, are the picturesque ruined walls and gate of *Rougemont* (Red Hill) *Castle*, first built by the Conqueror, and razed by Parliament, when Fairfax took it in 1646, after a siege. This is one of the best points of view, and is the spot where Colonel Penruddock was beheaded by Cromwell, for his premature rising for the king. The Sessions House stands within the bounds; close to it is the fine elm walk of Northern-bay. Friar's Walk, Pennsylvania Hill, and Mount Radford also command good views. 'There be divers fair streets in Exeter (says Leland, in Henry VIII's time), but the High Street that goeth from the west to the east gate is the fairest.' The gates he saw are gone, but parts of the strong walls remain, from whence there are good prospects. Where the street falls suddenly, two or three dry bridges have been built (the iron bridge in North Street, for instance), to save the descent. Another of stone, in line with High and Fore Streets, crosses the river, which runs rather swiftly here. In High Street is the venerable-looking Guildhall, containing portraits of Charles I, Queen Henrietta Maria and her daughter, the Duchess of Orleans, General Monk (by Lely), George II, &c. Lempière was master of the *Grammar School* at St John's Hospital. The Theatre is on the site of old Bedford House, where the Duchess of Orleans was born in the civil war.

On the east, near High Street, stands the fine *Cathedral*, which, as usual is a cross 375 feet long, internally. It is mostly early English, but the Norman towers, 145 feet high, belong to an older edifice erected by the Bishop Warlewast, and half ruined in the siege of 1137, when King Stephen took the town. The nave, choir, &c., were rebuilt as we see them now, between 1281 and 1420. Bishop Grandison's west front is perhaps the most striking part. It has been lately, restored, and is full of statues of kings, bishops, and scripture characters in niches. The window is also stained with a profusion of figures and coats of arms. The vault of the nave deserves notice. In the north tower is the great Peter bell, weighing five-and-a-half tons; ascend this tower for the view. A lady chapel, 56 feet by 30, is of the fourteenth century. The bishop's throne is of beautiful carved oak, 52 feet high, and as old as 1470. Among the monuments are Humphrey Bohun, Bishop Bronescombe (1280),

Bishop Stafford, the Courtenays, &c., and a fine one to Northcote, the painter, by Chantrey. The *Chapter House* is Gothic, 50 feet by 30, with a carved timber roof, and contains a library of 8,000 vols. A ship canal brings vessels up to the quay, where there is a very considerable trade carried on. Some of the best cider is made in the environs.

Excursions may be made from this point to Crediton, the original seat of the bishopric; Heavitree where Richard Hooker was born; Topsham, Powderham Castle (Earl of Devon), and Exmouth, down the Exe; over the Haldon Downs to Chudleigh and Ugbrook (Lord Clifford); Exmouth, Sidmouth, Dawlish, Teignmouth, and Torquay, and other beautiful spots along the coast; *Bicton*, seat of Lady Rolle, near Hayes Farm, where *Raleigh* was born. The entire coast of Devonshire is, perhaps, the most attractive in England.

Bude – a small port and picturesque village in the north-eastern extremity of Cornwall – has, within the last half-dozen years, risen to the dignity of a fashionable marine resort, to which distinction the excellent facilities it affords to bathers, and the picturesque scenery of its environs, have in a great measure contributed. The bed of the harbour, which is dry at low water, is composed of a fine bright yellow sand, chiefly consisting of small shells. The sea view is of a striking, bold, and sublime description – the rocks rising on every side to lofty broken elevations; and those who deserve a sequestered and romantic retreat will find in Bude the very object of their wish. The Bude Canal was commenced in 1819, and completed in 1826, at a cost of £128,000. It terminates within three miles of Launceston, forming an internal communication through Devon and Cornwall of nearly forty miles. Bude is fifty-two miles from Exeter.

The Exeter and Exmouth railway is now open, and runs via the stations of TOPSHAM, WOODBURY ROAD, and LYMPSTONE. The route here described, however, is by the old coach road, which, by the lover of the picturesque and the still lingering fascinations connected with the old mode of travelling, may have its superior attractions.

Passing through Topsham the road is studded with those charming old-fashioned villages that still linger in all their primitive simplicity along the western coast. From a hill called Beacon Hill, encountered in the progress, the eye is presented with a line of coast extending from Exeter to the southern boundary of Torbay, Berry Head, a distance of about twenty miles. This line is broken by several hills that ascend gradually from the opposite side of the river, clad with verdure to the summit, and sheltering the little village of Starcross in a wooden enclosure beneath. Mamhead and Poderham Castle, the seat of the Earl of Devon, heightened the beauty of the prospect, which is additionally embellished by the noble buildings connected with those estates.

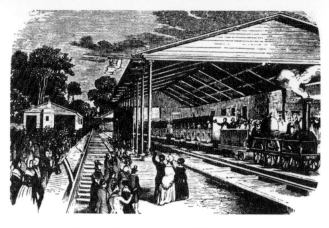

Exeter St Davids
The station at Exeter St Davids opened on 1 May 1844 and this event marked the completion of the seventy-six miles of railway from Bristol to Exeter. Typically, Brunel had laid out the station on the single-sided design with departure and arrivals platforms end on to each other. The distinctive broad gauge rails are clearly visible in this engraving.

Above: B&ER broad gauge loco No. 44 was designed by the company's engineer, James Pearson and was built by Rothwell & Co., of Bolton, in 1854. These massive 4-2-4T locos featured huge 9 foot driving wheels.

Right: Evidence of broad gauge times in this rail fence post in Somerset. It is not unusual to find discarded rail reused in this fashion throughout the former broad gauge network.

EXMOUTH.

A telegraph station.

This place has, within the last few years, made rapid strides in the march of improvement. The Beacon Hill is covered with buildings, and the Parade is stretching away right and left, with no visible signs, hitherto, of limitation.

Situated on the eastern side of the river Exe, two projecting sand banks form a partial enclosure, leaving an opening of about one-third the width of the harbour. The Exe is here about a mile and a half across, and though the entrance is somewhat difficult, the harbour is very convenient, and will admit the passage of ships of more than 300 tons burden.

There are two good inns, numerous boarding-houses and apartments, and a good subscription library and reading-room, but the visitor must create his own amusement, chiefly in the rides or pedestrian excursions, which the beauty of the surrounding country will so well afford the opportunity of enjoying. The proper time for bathing here is at high water, but there are hot and cold baths that can be taken at any hour, conveniently situated under the Beacon Terrace. Like many other maritime towns in Devonshire, Exmouth has in its immediate neighbourhood a valley sheltered on all sides from the winds, and capable of affording a genial retreat to those affected with complaints in the lungs. This will be found at Salterton, four miles to the east, and here the romantic caverns of the secluded bay, the rough but richly-pebbled beach, and the continuous marine prospect, will form irresistible temptations to explore the way thither. Dr. Clarke says, in speaking of the climate – 'Exmouth is decidedly a healthy place, and notwithstanding the whole of this coast is rather humid, agues are almost unknown.' Invalids often experience the greatest benefit from a residence here, most particularly on the Beacon Hill, the most elevated and finest situation in the neighbourhood, and which, as some compensation for the south-west gales, commands one of the most magnificent views in Devonshire. Along the southern base of the hill there is also a road of considerable extent, protected from the north and north-east winds, and well suited for exercise when they prevail; and here it may be remarked, that between the summer climate of North and South Devon there is as marked a difference as between the cast of their scenery, the air of the former being keen and bracing, and its features romantic and picturesque, while in the latter the rich softness of the landscape harmonizes with the soft and soothing qualities of the climate. An omnibus runs twice a week from Exmouth to Sidmouth.

About a mile from Exmouth is the secluded and picturesque village of Withycombe, and two miles further a fine old ruin, known as the Church of St John in the Wilderness, will attract attention. It was built

63

probably in the reign of Henry VII, but the old tower, one of the aisles, and part of the pulpit, now alone remain.

Sidmouth, eleven miles from Exmouth, is one of the most agreeably-situated little watering-places that can be imagined. It lies nestled in the bottom of a valley, opening to the sea between two lofty hills, 500 feet high, whence a most extensive and varied prospect of a beautiful part of the country is afforded on one side, and on the other a view of the open sea, bounded by a line of coast which stretches from Portland isle, on the east, to Torbay, on the west. The summit of Peak Hill on the west, is a lofty ridge, extending from north to south; that of Salcombe Hill, on the east, is much broader, and affords room for a race-course: both are highest towards the sea, where they terminate abruptly, forming a precipice of great depth, on the very verge of which the labourer may be seen guiding the plough several hundred feet perpendicular above the sea.

Although Sidmouth is irregularly built, its appearance is generally neat, occasionally highly picturesque, and in some parts positively handsome. The magnificent villas and cottages on the slopes are, almost without exception, surrounded with gardens; they command pleasing prospects and are delightfully accessible by shady lanes, which wind up the hills, and intersect each other in all directions. Old local topographers speak of Sidmouth as a considerable fishing town, and as carrying on some trade with Newfoundland, but its harbour is now totally choked up with rocks, which at low water are seen covered with seaweed, stretching away to a considerable distance from the shore. Its history may be briefly recounted. The manor of Sidmouth was presented by William the Conqueror to the Abbey of St Michel in Normandy, and was afterwards taken possession of by the Crown, during the wars with France, as the property of an alien foundation. It was afterwards granted to the monastery of Sion, with which it remained until the dissolution.

Hotels, boarding and lodging-houses are scattered over every part of Sidmouth and its vicinity, and the local arrangements are throughout excellent. The public buildings are soon enumerated, for they only consist of a church, near the centre of the town, a very ordinary edifice of the fifteenth century, enlarged from time to time, a neat little chapel of ease, and a new market-house, built in 1840. Around here, and in the Fore-street, are some excellent shops, and the town is well supplied with gas and water. The sea wall was completed in 1838. There was formerly an extensive bank of sand and gravel, thrown up by the sea, a considerable distance from the front of the town, but this being washed away in a tremendous storm, this defence was resorted to as a more permanent protection from the encroachment of the waves. It now forms an agreeable promenade, upwards of 1,700 feet long.

Sidmouth is sheltered by its hills from every quarter, except the south, where it is open to the sea, and has an atmosphere strongly impregnated with saline particles. Snow is very rarely witnessed, and in extremely severe seasons, when the surrounding hills are deeply covered, not a vestige, not a flake, will remain in this warm and secluded vale. The average mean winter temperature is from four to five degrees warmer than London, and eight degrees warmer than in the northern watering-places.

'In Sidmouth and its neighbourhood' (says the author of the 'Route Book of Devon'), 'will be found an inexhaustible mine for the study and amusement of the botanist, geologist, or conchologist. A very curious relic of antiquity was found on the beach here about five years since – a Roman bronze standard or centaur, representing the centaur Chiron, with his pupil Achilles behind his back. The bronze is cast hollow, and is about nine inches in height. The left fore leg of the centaur is broken, and the right hind leg mutilated. The under part or pedestal formed a socket, by which the standard was screwed on a pole or staff.'

The present great features of interest in the neighbourhood are the landslips, ten miles distant, which, extending along the coast from Sidmouth to Lyme Regis, are most interesting to the geologist and the lover of nature.

The range of cliffs, extending from Haven to Pinhay, has been the theatre of two convulsions, or landslips, one commencing on Christmas-day, 1839, at Bredon and Dowlands, whereby forty-five acre of arable land were lost to cultivation – the other about five weeks after, on the 3rd of February, 1840, at Whitlands, little more than a mile to the eastward of the former, but much smaller in magnitude than the previous one.

There are one or two situations, says an excellent local authority, overlooking the more western or great landslip, which seems to be admired as peculiarly striking – the view of the great chasm, looking eastward, and the view from Dowlands, looking westward, upon the undercliff and new beach. The best prospect, perhaps, for seeing the extraordinary nature of the whole district, combined with scenery, is from Pinhay and Whitlands, and looking inland you see the precipitous yet wooded summit of the main land, and the castellated crags of the ivy-clad rocks, on the terraces immediately below, and the deep dingle which separates you from it. By turning a little to the north-east Pinhay presents its chalky pinnacles and descending terraces; whilst to the west the double range and high perpendicular cliffs of Rowsedown offer themselves. By turning towards the sea is embraced the whole range of the great bay of Dorset and Devon, extending from Portland in the east to Start Point on the west, bounded on either side by scenery of the finest coast character.

The 'Atmospheric Caper'

Brunel had such faith in the atmospheric system of propulsion that he persuaded the directors of the South Devon Railway to adopt it for their line. This section of preserved pipe is on display at the Didcot Railway Centre. A piston moved through the pipe, sucked along by a semi-vacuum, connected through the slot to the carriages. Unfortunately leather flaps intended to seal the slot either perished or were eaten by the local rat population.

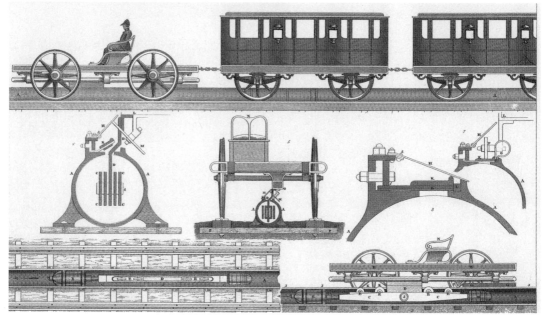

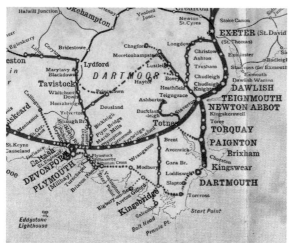

The plan was to build eleven pumping stations on the route between Exeter and Totnes. The atmospheric trains began in February 1848, but when it became clear that Brunel's great experiment was a failure, all operations ceased in September of the same year. Three of the pumping stations have survived in a recognisable form; at Starcross, Torquay and at Totnes.

South Devon Railway

Exeter to Torquay and Plymouth

This part of the line is invested with additional interest, from the magnificent scenery which opens on each side as we proceed. There is scarcely a mile traversed which does not unfold some peculiar picturesque charm or new feature of its own to make the eye 'dazzled and drunk with beauty'.

Once at Exeter, we have all the romantic allurements of the watering places of the west within our reach, where the possessor of robust health may find a fund of illimitable enjoyment in the rich bouquet that nature has spread before him on the freshening shores of Devon, and the invalid, those desired qualifications most conductive to a speedy and permanent convalescence.

On leaving Exeter we pass in rapid succession the stations of ST. THOMAS, EXMINSTER and STAR CROSS, and in a very few minutes arrive at

DAWLISH.
> Population, 3,505.
> A telegraph station.
> HOTELS – London; Royal.

DAWLISH, one of the stations of the South Devon Railway, is one of the prettiest places along the coast to pass a quiet summer month. Within the last century, rising from a mere fishing village to the dignity of a fashionable watering-place, it has become extended from the valley from which it lies to a considerable distance east and west; and though the incursion of the railroad has materially affected the fine expanse of the esplanade, it still possesses an excellent beach, bounded on the east by the Langstone Cliffs, and on the west by the rocks familiarly known by the appellation of the Parson and Clerk. The bathing is exceedingly good, and the facilities afforded for its enjoyment admirably arranged. The houses, built in handsome terraces along the side of the hill and strand, and fronted by lawns and gardens, are very and some and picturesque, the majority of them commanding an ample sea view. The parish church is at the upper end of the town, and was partly rebuilt in 1824, being rendered sufficiently commodious to accommodate a congregation of nearly two thousand people. There is a good organ, and a handsome window of stained glass in the interior.

The walks and drives in the vicinity of the town are remarkably

Starcross and Dawlish

Top left: A truncated chimney rises above the former atmospheric pumping station at Starcross, sandwiched between the road and the railway line.

Top right: The dilapidated signal box on Dawlish station.

Left: The railway line cuts Dawlish off from the beach, with only a low underpass linking the two. Brunel chose this coastal route as the most viable way to circumnavigate hillier terrain inland.

Bottom left: The sea wall, shown here to the east of Dawlish, was built to protect this exposed section of line from the elements. Brunel's single broad gauge line has given way to a double track and the later sea wall is composed of limestone masonry which is filled in behind with hard rubble.

pretty and interesting, the shady lanes at the back, winding through the declivity of the hills, affording an endless variety of inland and marine scenery. The climate is considered more genial than even that of Torquay; but so nearly do these places approximate that, for all general purposes, the remarks made upon the atmospheric characteristics of Torquay will be found equally applicable to those of Dawlish. Of late years, considerable improvement has been effected in the watching and lighting arrangements of the town, and some new buildings have added much to its external beauty. A new church in the Gothic style, St Mark's, has recently been erected. Circulating libraries and hotels, with the other usual accessories to a fashionable marine resort, are numerous and well provided, and the excursionist may here crown the enjoyments of the day with such a stroll on the beach by moonlight as can be obtained at few other places. One of the most delightful excursions in the neighbourhood is to *Luscombe Park*, the seat of – Hoare, Esq. Good facilities for boating and fishing by applying to Coombe, a trustworthy old seaman.

TEIGNMOUTH.

POPULATION, 6,022.
A telegraph station.
HOTELS – Royal; Devon.

TEIGNMOUTH, three miles from Dawlish, is recognised as the largest watering place on the Devonian coast; but, from the irregularity of the streets, it is only in the esplanade that it can rival the others before named. A large export trade is carried on here, which gives a life and animation to the streets, and the bustle that occasionally prevails is often felt as an agreeable change to the monotony of a country-residence. The air is more bracing and considerably colder than at Dawlish or Torquay, the town being much exposed to the east winds. In respect to both the excellence and accommodation of houses and apartments, there are few places more convenient for either a temporary or permanent residence than Teignmouth. An excellent supply of gas and water is enjoyed by the town, and all the comforts, with most of the luxuries, of life are easily and economically obtainable. There are two churches, situated respectively in East and West Teignmouth, the former being the more modern, and the latter – particularly as regards the interior – being the more interesting. The Assembly Rooms, with Subscription, Reading, Billiard, and News Rooms attached, furnish an agreeable source of amusement, and libraries are, with hotels, plentifully scattered through the town.

The river Teign, which here flows into the Channel, yields an abundant supply of fish, and the pleasure of a sail up the river to the interior is to be numbered among the allurements of a sojourn. A bridge, considered the longest in England, has been thrown across the Teign at this point,

Sea Wall perils

Left: This classic GWR publicity photograph of the Cornish Riviera Express passing the sea wall with Dawlish in the background. But in December 1852 part of the cliff near Breeches Rock, between Dawlish and Teignmouth, gave way after heavy rain and brought down a section of the sea wall. Passengers were stranded and had to make their way climbing around the foot of the cliffs.

Below: At Teignmouth the railway turns inland and away from the sea wall. *(LoC)*

erected in 1827, at a cost of nearly £20,000. It is 1,672 feet in length, and consists of thirty-four arches, with a drawbridge over the deepest part of the channel, to allow free passage of vessels.

Near the mouth of the river is a lighthouse exhibiting a red light. The noble esplanade – or Teignmouth *Den*, as it is curiously styled – is a deservedly favourite promenade with all visitors, and the bold and towering cliffs that overhang the sea impart a most romantic aspect to the surrounding scenery. Excursions either on sea or land may be made from Teignmouth with the greatest facility of conveyance, and the environs are so extremely rich in natural and artificial attractions that they are almost inexhaustible. Three fairs are held in the months of January, February, and September, and an annual regatta takes place in August. The post-office is in Bank Street.

NEWTON JUNCTION.
(Newton Abbots).

> Telegraph station at Teignmouth, 5 miles.
> HOTEL – Globe.
> MARKET DAY – Wednesday.
> FAIRS – Last Wednesday in Feb., June 24th, first Wednesday in Sept., and Nov. 6th.

Here is a stone where William of Orange first read his declaration.

[TORQUAY AND DARTMOUTII BRANCH]

TOTNES.

> Population, 4,001.
> A telegraph station.
> MARKET DAY – Saturday.
> FAIRS – First Tuesday in every month, Easter Tuesday, May 12th, and October 1st.

TOTNES is situated on the river Dart. The ancient Roman fosseway forms a prominent feature in this town. There is a good deal of woollen cloth manufactured here, but the chief employment of the inhabitants is in the fishery. Its principal attractions are a Guildhall, assembly room and theatre, banks, libraries, &c.

After a very brief stoppage at BRENT and KINGS-BRIDGE ROAD stations we arrive at

IVY BRIDGE.
A charming spot in the valley of the Erme, much frequented in summer. The hills (1,000 feet high at one point) here begin to ascend towards *Dartmoor*, which lies to the north-west. It is a desolate tract of

granite moorland, twenty miles long by twelve broad, once a forest, but now covered with peat. Copper and tin are worked. Some of its rugged peaks, here called tors, are 1,200 to 2,000 feet high; and under one is the Dartmoor Convict Prison. The Dart rises at Cranmere; on account of its striking scenery and fishing, it should be descended all the way to the fine port of Dartmouth.

CORNWOOD and PLYMPTON stations.

PLYMOUTH.

A telegraph station.

HOTELS – Royal Hotel; Chubbs' Commercial.

FLY CHARGES – For two persons, any distance not exceeding one mile, 8d.; every additional half-mile, 4d. For three or four persons per mile, or fraction of a mile, 1s.; every additional half-mile, 6d. Nor fare, however, to be less than 1s.

BANKERS – Branch of the Bank of England; Harris & Co.; Devon and Cornwall Banking Co.

A borough, first class fortress, and naval dockyard in *Devonshire*, at the north of the Channel, 246 miles from London by the Great Western Railway. The dockyard and harbour are at Devonport, the victualling office is at Stonehouse, and there are other establishments in the neighbourhood, but Plymouth is the common name for all. Two members. Population 62,599. The view from the Hoe, or cliffy height on which the *Citadel* is planted, commands a magnificent prospect of the sound or outer anchorage, Mounts Batten and Edgecumbe hedging it in on both sides, and the breakwater which protects the main entrance. Two rivers run into the sound, the Plym on the east side, and the Tamar on the west, or Devonport. The mouth of the first, on which Plymouth stands, widens into a deep inlet called the Catwater. Close to the town is Sutton pool, a tide-harbour in which vessels of various tonnage lie. About 35,000 tons of shipping are registered at this port, and the total amount of customs may be stated at £10,000. It is a convenient starting point for emigrants, for whom a depot has been established.

There is a tower, and some other remains of a castle, on the Hoe, which was first gradually fortified in 1670. Here are the new botanic gardens. The climate of this part of Devonshire is somewhat moist, but it keeps up a perpetual verdure to make amends.

Some of the best buildings are designed by Foulston, who died in 1842. This architect built the Public Library, in 1812; the Exchange, in 1813; and the Athenæum, in 1819. But his first and largest works were the Assembly Rooms, Royal Hotel and Theatre, in one immense block in the Ionic style, 270 feet by 220; built 1811, for the corporation. Foulston also restored the old *Parish Church* of St Andrew, in which is a monument to C. Matthews, the comedian. Its bell tolls the curfew *couvrez feu*, or 'put out fire', every night, striking according to the days of the month. At the *Guildhall* is a portrait of Sir F. Drake, its most eminent native, who was at the cost of cutting a stream, twenty-four miles long, from Dartmoor, to supply the Town reservoir. Christ Church is a modern Gothic church, by Wightwick, who also designed the new *Post Office*, in the Grecian style.

At the western extremity of the town is Mill Bay, where Docks have been formed for the Great Western Packet Station. On the side of Stonehouse (which, though one town with Plymouth, is part of Devonport borough) are the Naval and Military Hospital, the Marine Barracks, and the Victualling Office, the last a solid granite quadrangle, which cost one and a-half million sterling. It occupies a site of fifteen acres, and includes biscuit baking machinery, cooperage, and immense provision stores. Line-of-battle ships can come alongside the quay.

EXCURSIONS FROM PLYMOUTH. – These are almost endless in variety, and equally beautiful. The visitor will be soon made acquainted with clotted cream, junket, white pot, squab pie, and other west country mysteries, and the unbounded hospitality of the people. Within a few miles are the following: *Mount-Edgecumbe* (on the Cornwall side of the Sound), the seat of Earl Mount-Edgecumbe, in a beautiful park, overlooking Plymouth, the breakwater, sea, &c. A fort in the Sound was

Heading westwards out of Totnes the line swings across the hilly terrain of South Devon. This is Ivybridge with the high viaduct in the background, *c.* 1900. As with the Cornish viaducts this was one of Brunel's timber structures originally. *(LoC)*

Plymouth and Devonport
The Great Western Dock Company employed Brunel to oversee the dock-works at Millbay, *left*. He also designed a floating pontoon pier head for steam ships, and had submitted plans for a gated dock at Sutton Pool, although these were rejected by the Admiralty.

Built in 1810 *HMS Impregnable* was a second-rate three-decker that was rated as a training ship in 1862 and moored at Devonport for the training of boys entering the Royal Navy.

Right, the launch of an ironclad at the Devonport dockyards in 1863.

first built when the Armada invaded these shores; and it was from this port that Howard of Effingham, Drake, and Hawkins, sailed out to attack it. *Deus afflavit, et dissipantur*; and where is Spain now! Maker Church, 300 or 400 feet high, is the best point for enjoying the prospect. Below is the Ram Head of the ancient geographers, and still called Rame, and Whitsand Bay, a rare spot for seaweed and shells. Fine creeks and bays hence to the Land's End. On the Cornish side, also, are – *East Anthony*, the old seat of the Carews; *Thancks*, Dowager Lady Graves, and St German's Norman Church, near *Port Eliot*, the seat of Earl St. Germans. It contains part of a priory founded by King Athelstane. On the Devonshire side of Plymouth are – *Saltram*, Earl Morley's seat; good pictures by Reynolds, &c. Boringdon was their old seat, higher up the Catwater. *Newnham Park*, G. Strode Esq. *Plympton* (five miles), a decayed borough, the birthplace of Sir J. Reynolds, whose portrait, by himself, is in the Guildhall. Traces of a castle. *Yealimpton, Modbury, Kingsbridge*, &c., are on the various creeks of South Devon, which increase in beauty towards Dartmouth and Torquay; most of the streams come from Dartmoor. Fruit &c., are abundant in this mild and fertile region.

Up the Tamar. This beautiful stream divided the two counties for some miles. Past *St Budeaux* (on the right, or Devonshire side), a fine spot, opposite Saltash. Then *Landulph* (on the left) where Theodore Palæolipus, the survivor of the last Emperor of Constantinople, is buried. The tomb was opened about 1830. One of his daughters married an Arundell, of *Clifton*, an old seat here. Lead mines here, and at *Beer Ferris* (Devon side), which is charmingly placed on the corner where the Tavy runs past *Buckland Abbey* (fragments of a priory), the seat of Sir T. T. Drake, Bart., a descendant of the great navigator, who was born at Tavistock. This is the centre of an important mining district, with some remains of an abbey, belonging to the Bedford family. Following the Tamar, you come to *Pentilie* (J. Coryton Esq.), and Cothele, both on the Cornwall side. The latter seat, for centuries in the Edgecumbe family, is one of the most interesting in England, for its architecture, furniture, and ornaments, all genuine relics of a mediæval age. *Callington*, to the left, near *St Kitt's Hill*, the granite peak of *Hengstown Down*, 1,067 feet high, from the summit of which there is a famous prospect. The river winds hence to Launceton.

The Royal Albert Bridge

Bradshaw makes no mention of the Royal Albert Bridge over the Tamar at Saltash. Yet this crossing was one of Brunel's greatest challenges and his greatest triumph. The Admiralty had required a bridge high enough to allow the passage of its tall-masted ships, but a conventional suspension bridge was unsuitable for a railway. Instead Brunel devised a 'closed system' with two great wrought iron tubes containing the compression forces combined with the tied suspension support chains. It was the natural successor to the railway bridge at Chepstow and, to my mind, the most spectacular of all his works. The Royal Albert Bridge was open by the Prince Consort on 2 May 1859. Brunel was too ill to attend the ceremony and he was taken across the bridge in an open-topped wagon. He died later that year.

Top left: The opening of the line seen from Saltash station on the Cornish side.

Second left: The bridge has recently undergone a major refurbishment and this photograph from the west shore of the Tamar was taken in 2012. The tent structures allow work to continue despite the weather conditions and help to prevent debris from falling into the river.
   As shown on Terence Cuneo's evocative cover artwork for the 1963 edition of the Triang model railway catalogue, the lines converge to a single track over the bridge. In the days before the road bridge was built alongside, it was not unknown for locals returning from a late night out in Plymouth to walk back across the railway bridge.

Lower left: The bright signs welcoming travellers to Cornwall screen the decrepit state of the old station building at Saltash.

Welcome to Cornwall
Kernow a'gas dynnergh

On Cornish Lines to Penzance

CORNWALL.

CORNWALL, from its soil, appearance, and climate, is one of the least inviting of the English counties. A ridge of bare and rugged hills, intermixed with bleak moors, runs through the midst of its whole length, and exhibits the appearance of a dreary waste. The most important objects in the history of this county are its numerous mines, which for centuries have furnished employment to its inhabitants; and the trade to which they give birth, when considered in a national point of view, is of the greatest relative consequence. In a narrow slip of land, where the purposes of agriculture would not employ above a few thousand inhabitants, the mines also support a population estimated at more than 80,000 labourers, exclusive of artisans. The principal produce of the Cornish mines is tin, copper, and lead. The strata in which these metals are found extend from the Land's End, in a direction from west to east, entirely along the county into Devonshire. Nearly all the metals are found in veins or fissures, the direction of which is generally east and west. The annual value of the copper mines has been estimated at £350,000. Logan stones deserve to be mentioned amongst the curiosities of this county. They are of great weight, and poised on the top of immense piles of rocks.

CORNWALL RAILWAY.

Plymouth to Truro.
Almost before we get clear of Plymouth our arrival is announced at

DEVONPORT
 (a telegraph station).

A place of great importance, partly overlooking the Sound (where it is defended by Mount Wise battery), and the anchorage at the Tamar's mouth, called *Hamaoze*. Here is the royal *Dockyard*, on a space of seventy-one acres, inclusive of five more at the Gun Wharf (built by Sir J. Vanburgh). The Dockyard includes various docks and building slips, storehouses, a rope house 200 fathoms long, blacksmiths' shop, &c. Above this is the floating bridge to Torpoint and the splendid *Steam*

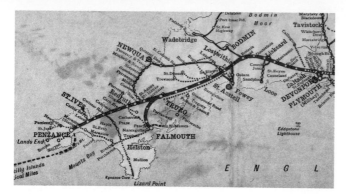

Into Cornwall
The route of the main line shown on a GWR map from the 1920s. It followed the lines of two companies, the Cornwall Railway as far as Truro and the West Cornwall Railway beyond.

As the line entered Cornwall it was carried aloft by a spectacular series of Brunel's timber viaducts, all of which have since been replaced. The first one, at Coombe-by-Saltash, is a spectacular viaduct in its own right but is overshadowed by the twin humps of the Royal Albert Bridge.

Right: Bradshaw described Cornwall as 'one of the least inviting of the English counties', but the coming of the railways was to bring tourists to the county by the trainload.

Docks and factory at Keyham, which occupy another seventy-five acres. There are two basins, 600 to 700 feet long, beside docks, all faced with solid stone, and built at a total cost of one and a half million, along with foundries, smithery, &c. One wrought-iron caisson is 82 feet long, and 13 feet thick. Devonport has a population of 64,783, and returns two members. A pillar opposite the Town hall was placed there in 1824, when the name was altered from Plymouth Dock. There are various barracks near Mount Wise, where the Governor of the district and the Port Admiral reside.

Plymouth Sound, and its three harbours, would hold, it is calculated, 2,000 vessels, such is its extent. One of the most striking scenes it has witnessed in modern times was the appearance of Napoleon here, in 1815, on board the Bellerophon, after his attempted escape to America. Across the mouth (having entrances on each side), three miles from the town, is the famous Breakwater, first begun in 1812, by Rennie. It is a vast stone dyke, gradually made by sinking 2 ½ million tons of stone, from the neighbouring cliffs; about 10 or 12 yards wide at the top, and spreading to 70 or 80 yards at the bottom – the side next to the Atlantic being the most sloping. Its entire length is 1,700 yards, nearly a mile; but it is not straight, as the two ends bend inwards from the middle part, which is 1,000 yards long. A lighthouse stands at the west corner, 63 feet high. Several tremendous storms have tested its solidity and usefulness; once inside this artificial bulwark, the smallest craft is as safe as if it were on the slips of the Dockyard.

The Eddystone Lighthouse is ten miles from it, on a granite rock in the open channel. It was erected by Mr. Smeaton, and is a striking instance of human ingenuity, which has hitherto baffled all the fury of the elements. The first stone was laid on the 1st of June, 1757. Mr. Smeaton conceived the idea of his edifice from the waist or bole of a large spreading oak. Considering the figure of the tree as connected with its roots, which lie hid below ground, Mr. S. observed that it rose from the surface with a large swelling base, which at the height of one diameter, is generally reduced by an elegant concave curve to a diameter less by at least one-third, and sometimes to half its original base. Hence he deducted what the shape of a column of the greatest stability ought to be to resist the action of external violence, when the *quantity of matter* of which it is to be composed is given. To expedite the erection of the building, the stones were hewn and fitted to each other on shore, and after every precaution to ensure security had been taken, the work was completed in October, 1759. It has proved highly beneficial to all nations, which fact was strikingly exemplified by Louis XIV. France being at war with England while the lighthouse was being proceeded with, a French privateer took the men at work on the Eddystone rocks, together with their tools, and carried them to France, the captain expecting a reward for the achievement. While the captives

Eddystone

The one piece of civil engineering that most attracted Bradshaw's attention was the very one that his readers were least likely to visit. The building of the Eddystone Lighthouse, on an isolated granite rock, had been a marvel of its time. The first one, an octagonal structure completed in 1698, was swept away by the great storm of 1703 and replaced by John Smeaton's granite 'Tower' in 1759. When this weakened it was dismantled, leaving the stump, and rebuilt on Plymouth Hoe. The present one was designed by Robert Stevenson following Smeaton's principles and is now a fully automated lighthouse and capped by a helipad.

lay in prison the transaction came to the knowledge of the French monarch, who immediately ordered the prisoners to be released and the captors to be confined to their stead, declaring that though he was at war with England he was not so with mankind. He therefore directed the men to be sent back to their work with presents.

The form of the present lighthouse is octagonal, and the framework is composed of cast iron and copper. The outside and basement of the edifice are formed of granite, that kind of stone being more competent than any other to resist the action of the sea. Round the upper store-room, upon the course of granite under the ceiling, is the following inscription:

'Except the Lord build the house,
They labour in vain that build it.'

Over the east side of the lantern are the words – '24th August, 1759. Laus Deo.'

The number of keepers resident at the lighthouse was at first only two, but an incident of a very extraordinary and distressing nature which occurred showed the necessity of an additional hand. One of the two keepers took ill and died. The dilemma in which this occurrence left the survivor was singularly painful: apprehension that if he tumbled the dead body into the sea, which was the only way in his power to dispose of it, he might be charged with murder, he was induced for some time to let the corpse lie, in hopes that the attending-boat might be able to land, and relieve him from the distress he was in. By degrees the body became so putrid that it was not in his power to get quit of it without help, for it was near a month before the boat could effect a landing.

Since the above occurrence three men have been stationed at Eddystone, each of whom has, in the summer, a month's leave to visit his friends, and are provided with food and all other necessities by a boat appointed for the purpose; but they are always stocked with salt provisions, to guard against the possibility of want, as in winter it sometimes happens that the boat cannot approach the rock for many weeks together. The range of the enjoyments of the keepers is confined within very narrow limits. In high winds so briny an atmosphere surrounds this gloomy solitude, from the dashing of the waves, that a person exposed to it could hardly draw his breath. At these dreadful intervals the forlorn inhabitants keep close quarters, and are obliged to live in darkness, listening to the howling storm, excluded in every emergency from the help of human assistance, and without any earthly comfort but that which results from their confidence in the strength of the building in which they are immured. In fine weather they just

Menheniot

The Coldrennick Viaduct at Menheniot was one of fifty-four timber viaducts in the county, including the main line itself and the branch to Falmouth. These had all been capped or replaced with masonry/steel structures by the early 1930s.

St Germans

Above: The 945 foot viaduct at St Germans. Built in 1859 it was replaced by the present masonry structure in 1907.

Right: One of several old railway carriages being renovated at the former St Germans' station to provide holiday accommodation.

scramble about the edge of the rock when the tide ebbs, and amuse themselves with fishing; and this is the only employment they have, except that of trimming their nightly fires. Singular as it may appear, there are yet facts which lead us to believe it possible for these men to become enamoured of their situation. Smeaton, in speaking of one of these light-keepers says,

'In the fourteen years that he had been here he was grown so attached to the place, that for two summers preceding he had given up his turn on shore to his companions, and declared his intention of doing the same the third, but was over-persuaded to go on shore and take his month's turn. He had always in this service proved himself a decent, sober, well-behaved man; but he had no sooner got on shore than he went to an alehouse and got intoxicated. This he continued the whole of his stay, which being noticed, he was carried, in this intoxicated state, on board the Eddystone boat, and delivered to the lighthouse, where he was expected to grow sober; but after lingering two or three days, he could by no means be recovered.'

In another place he says,

'I was applied to by a philosopher kind of a man to be one of the light-keepers, observing, that being a man of study and retirement, he could very well bear the confinement that must attend it. I asked him if he knew of the salary? He replied no; but doubted not it must be something very handsome. When I told him it was £25 a-year, he replied he had quite mistaken the business; he did not mean to sell his liberty for so low a price; he could not have supposed it less than three times as much.'

Another man, a shoemaker, who was engaged to be the light-keeper, when in the boat which conveyed him thither, the skipper addressing him, said, 'How happens it, friend Jacob, that you should choose to go and be cooped up here as a light-keeper, when you can on shore, as I am told, earn half-a-crown and three shillings in a-day in making leathern hose (leathern pipes so called), whereas the light-keeper's salary is but £25 a-year, which is scarce ten shillings a-week?' 'Everyone to his taste,' replied Jacob promptly; 'I go to be a light-keeper because I don't like confinement.' After this answer had produced its share of merriment, Jacob explained himself by saying that he did not like to be confined to work.

From Davenport we resume our journey, passing the stations of SALTASH, ST. GERMANS, MENHENIOT, LISKEARD, DOUBLEBOIS, and BODMIN ROAD.

Change of gauge...
The line from Paddington to Penzance was built to Brunel's broad gauge, but delays were caused when it met the narrower gauge used elsewhere. These illustrations show the chaos of transferring passengers and goods from one train to another.

Right: One answer to the change of gauge issue was the transfer shed. This example at the GWS railway centre at Didcot has the narrower or standard gauge on the left side, and the broad gauge track on the left. The central platform is not very wide to ease the changeover between the trains.

84

...and changing the gauge

The incompatibility of alternative gauges was recognised as a hindrance to the smooth running of the rapidly expanding railway network. In 1846 a Royal Commission set up to examine the issue came down in favour of the narrower standard gauge.

Right: One temporary solution had been the construction of mixed gauge track, as shown here on this reconstructed section at Didcot. It is a clear indication of the difference between the 4 foot 8 inch gauge favoured by the Stephenson's in the north of the country and Brunel's wider 7 foot gauge. Just imagine today's railways if it had been the broad gauge that had won this 'battle of the gauges'.

In May 1892 the last of the broad gauge track was ripped up in a mammoth operation. The middle image shows navvies at work at Saltash – compare this scene with the one on page 76.

Although the fate of the broad gauge had been sealed during Brunel's lifetime, he died in 1859 and consequently did not live to see its final passing. As a mark of respect *Punch* published this illustration of his ghost passing by as the navvies laid the broad gauge to rest.

St Austell station and viaduct

Postcard view looking west from the road bridge. St Austell station opened in May 1859 on the Cornwall Railway and made the town an important commercial centre for the area's china clay industry. It is now the main rail link for visitors to the Eden Project. *(CMcC)*

Below: The proximity of the houses around the St Austell viaduct on the west side of the town makes it seem even more imposing. Note the familiar row of original piers.

LOSTWITHIEL.

A telegraph station.

The only features of attraction here are the parish church and the ruins of a building called the palace. The former was built in the fourteenth century, has a fine spire and a curious font. The latter is said to have been the residence of the Dukes of Cornwall.

PAR station.

ST. AUSTELL, or St. Austle

A telegraph station.

A large mining town in West Cornwall, near the sea, with several important mines round it in the granite, producing tin, copper, nickel, with clay, and china stone, for the Staffordshire potteries. Good building stone is also quarried. Graw or stratum is the most valuable product, found in round masses, and smelted in the neighbourhood. The chief mines are Polgooth, Crinnis, Pentewan, &c.; there are only one or two of copper. Tram rails have been made to the little harbour of Pentewan, and Charlestown, in the bay, to ship the ores. Among the buildings are several chapels, a stannery (or tin) hall, and an ancient stone church with a good tower, on which, and over the south porch of the church, are various carvings. Population, 3,825.

The tin mines which were worked in Cornwall by the roving Phœnicians long before Christ, yield here, and at St. Agnes, &c., about 5,000 tons, worth £70 a ton, yearly. Copper, now the staple article of the county, used to thrown aside by the tinners, till the beginning of the last century. Polgooth, a tine mine, two miles south-west, in a barren spot, is now almost worked out; formerly it was worth £20,000 a year. It is 120 fathoms deep. Crinnis, which was worth between £80,000 or £90,000 is still very productive in copper. At Carclaze the tin is worked in the light granite of the downs, by lateral shafts, open to the day.

COMPOUND ROAD – About two miles from this station is the rotton borough of Grampound, one of the many existing in Cornwall (which, being a crown duchy, the court influence was the paramount), but disfranchised for gross corruption, in 1841.

TRURO.

Distance from station, 1 mile.

A telegraph station.

HOTEL – Red Lion.

MARKET DAYS – Wednesday after Mid-Lent, Wednesday in Whitsun week, November 19th, December 8th.

10758. - TRURO. GENERAL VIEW.

Truro, Railway Viaduct

The City of Truro
Truro has not one but two viaducts with the station located on the hill between them. On the east side the Truro viaduct of 1,329 feet sits on twenty piers, while on the other side of town the Carvedras viaduct runs for a further 969 feet on fifteen piers. (*LoC*)

Left, postcard *c.* 1900 showing the Carvedas viaduct with its timber superstructure still in use, and *below*, a recent view of the replacement viaduct and abandoned piers at Truro.

TRURO, the mining capital of Cornwall, and a parliamentary borough (two members). Its population is 11,337 within the borough bands, which enclose a space of 1,200 acres, at the head of a creek of the Fal (where the rivers Kenwyn and Allen fall in), covered by foundries, blast houses, pottery and tin works &c. When the tide is up the creek looks like a fine lake, two miles long. Like most Cornish towns, Truro originated by a castle built by the Earls of Cornwall, on Castle Hill. It is now the principal coinage town in the Duchy, where the metal is stamped, previous to being exported. Bar tin is sent to the Mediterranean, &c., and ingots to the East Indies, while much of the copper ore is taken across to Swansea.

The principal streets diverge from the market place, near which is St Mary's Church, a handsome later Gothic edifice, with a tower. It contains various monuments to old Truro families. There are two other churches, beside one at Kenwyn, north of the town, near the county infirmary. The *Coinage Hall* is an old building, formerly used as a stannary parliament, i.e., a parliament of tinners (*stannum*, tin). Town Hall, built in 1615. Theatre and Assembly Room, at High Cross. A good museum at the Royal Institute of Cornwall. Attempts have been made to establish a mining college, chiefly by the liberal exertions of Sir C. Lemon, after whom Lemon Street, on the Falmouth Road, takes its name. At the top of it is a *pillar* to the African travellers, Richard and J. Lander, natives of Truro, the latter of whom perished on this third trip to that insalubrious coast.

Within a short distance are the following places, mostly seated on the Fal or its branches. *Polwhele* was the seat of Polwhele the antiquary, a member of an ancient Cornish family. 'By Tre, Pol, and Pen, you may know the Cornishmen,' is a well known thyme. *Pencarlnich*, seat of J. Vivian, Esq. – another old name. *Tregothnan*, the seat of the Earl of Falmouth, a beautiful spot. Here Admiral Boscawen was born, in 1711. *Trewarthenich*, another fine seat, near Tregony, *Trelissich*, on the west side of the Fal. *Carclew*, near Penryn, the seat of Sir C. Lemon, Bart. Enys, of J. Enys Esq. *Trefusis*, beautifully placed opposite Falmouth, is the seat of Lord Clinton.

Falmouth was formerly an important mail packet station. Below it are Pendennis Castle and St. Anthony's Light, on the opposite sides of the entrance. The former, built by Henry VIII, was famous in the civil war for its resistance to parliament, against whose forces it held out till 1646. The richest mines are in the granite moorlands to the north, near St Agnes, &c., or in the neighbourhood of the rail to Penzance. At Perranzabulae, five miles from Truro, an ancient British church was uncovered, 25 feet in 1835, by shifting sands (which in former times overwhelmed everything on this side of the coast), and gave occasion to Mr. Trelawney's work, 'Lost Church Found', in which he shows what the primitive English church was before corrupted by Popery. This and other parishes were named from the famous St Tiran, the patron of

West Cornwall

The West Cornwall Railway continued the line westwards from Truro to Penzance and, in part, incorporated the route of the earlier Hayle Railway. In constructing the ten viaducts on this final leg Brunel favoured less masonry and more timber.

Top left: Hayle's relatively low-level viaduct is only 34 feet high, but it is over 800 feet long. As this photograph shows some of the replacement masonry piers have started to lean slightly out of line.

Lower three images: The station at Redruth is a charming survivor. Note the footbridge with GWR monograms – there is a similar one at St Austell. Immediately beyond Redruth station the line passes over the viaduct which was built in 1852 with short masonry piers and a fan of timber supports. Its replacement dates from 1888 and roughly follows the alignment of the original, and the remains of some of the old piers can be found.

tinners, who, like many other eminent preachers of that age, came from Ireland. The story is that he sailed over on a mill stone, but perhaps this was the name of the ship. Near St Agnes Beacon is a camp called Picran Round, Chacewater, Wheal Towan, Wheal Leisure, Pen Hale, Perran St George (all near Perran Porth, the last 100 fathoms deep); and Buduick mine may be visited, Polperro, Wheal Kitty Wheal Alfred and others, most of them indicative of the arbitary names conferred on mines by the lively fancy of the Cornishmen. Population, 4,953.

WEST CORNWALL RAILWAY

Truro to Hayle, Penzance &c.
CHACEWATER and SCORRIER GATE stations.

REDRUTH.
> POPULATION, 7,919.
> A telegraph station.
> HOTELS – London; King's Arms.
> MARKET DAY – Friday.
> FAIRS – May 2nd, July 9th, Sept. 5th, and Oct. 12th.

REDRUTH, is a market town, in the county of Cornwall. It consists of one long street, from which branch several smaller ones. This town derives nearly all its importance from its central situation with respect to the neighbouring mines, the working of which has increased the population to treble its original number, as nearly all the commercial transactions of the miners are carried on here.

On leaving Redruth, and passing the unimportant stations of POOL, CAMBORNE, GWINEAR ROAD, and HAYLE, we arrive at

ST IVES ROAD.
> Telegraph Station at Hayle, 1½ mile.

The town of St Ives has a population of 10,353, chiefly depending on the coasting trade and pilchard fishery. Treganna Castle, the seat of Mr. Stephens, occupies a lofty situation outside the town, and commands an extensive prospect.
> MARAZION ROAD station.

PENZANCE.
> A telegraph station.
> HOTELS – Union; Star.
> MARKET DAYS – Thursday and Saturday.
> FAIRS – Thursday before Advent, Thursday after Trinity

Destination Penzance
Left: the last of the timber viaducts, a low level structure along the shoreline leading to Penzance station. This engraving from *The Illustrated London News* shows the effects of violent storms. It has since been replaced by an embankment. St Michael's Mount is visible in the background.

A busy scene at Penzance station – the end of the line and the end of our journey. One of the coaches carries a sign for the GWR's Cornish Riviera Express, a creation of the GWR's marketing department.

Right: Mount's Bay and the tidal island of St Michael's Mount which Bradshaw described as 'most striking'.

Sunday, and Corpus Christi day.

BANKERS – Bolithos, Sons, and Co.; Batten, Carne, and Co.

This flourishing port is at the farther end of Cornwall, on the west side of Mount's Bay, at the terminus of the West Cornwall Railway. It is a municipal, but not a parliamentary borough, with a population of 9,414. Tin, copper, china, clay, granite, and pilchards are the principal articles of trade here. The harbour, enclosed by a pier, 600 feet long, is shallow, but it is easy to reach and get out of. All the best shops are in the Market Place, where the four principal streets centre. The stannery court for the hundred of Penwith is abolished. An excellent Geological Society was founded in 1813; and is enriched by a full collection of specimens obtained by Dr. Boase, from every corner of the county, and carefully arranged. The churches and houses are of stone. Madron is the mother church. Sir Humphrey Davy, the great chemist, was born at Penzance, 1778; after serving his apprenticeship to a chemist here, he went to assist Dr. Beddoes at the Pneumatic Institution. Penzance is a cheap and healthy place for a resident. The soil in the neighbourhood is light and rich, from the granite dust at the bottom, and produces uncommonly heavy crops of *potatoes*, the returns being 300 to 600 bushels an acre. Sand, shells, and pilchards, are used to manure it.

Mount's Bay, which is spread out before the town, is eighteen miles wide at the mouth, from the Lizard Point on the east, to the Rundlestone on the west side. The shore is low and uninteresting; but what geologists call raised beaches are seen. *St. Michael's Mount*, the most striking object in it, and to which it owes its name, is a conspicuous granite rock, four miles east of Penzance, about a quarter of a mile from the shore, off the town of Marazion. It is reached (at low water only) by a causeway, and stands 250 feet high. A few fishermen's cottages are round the base, and at the top are remains of a priory, founded before the Conquest, and for ages resorted to by pilgrims, whose rock is at the end of the causeway. Here the wife of the Pretender, Perkin Warbeck, found refuge in 1497. There are traces of a great variety of minerals; and it commands by far the best prospect of the bay. In olden times it was called *Ictes*, and was a tin depot. The flow of pilgrims to this point was the making of Marazion, which formerly possessed a good trade, but is now an insignificant town. *Marghasion* is its Cornish name, indicative probably of its position, and it being once held by Sion Abbey. Sometimes it is called Market-Jew, which is a corruption of another Cornish name, *Marghasjewe*.

Penzance is between the two districts which hem in the opposite sides of the bay, and from the tail end, as it were, of Cornwall, Kerrien towards the Lizard, and Penwith to the Land's End. Both possess a coast not very lofty, but broken and dangerous. They differ in their geological character – the Lizard district being mostly slaty or 'killas', and serpentine; and that of the Penwith, round the Land's End, granite here called moorstone. Penwith signifies, in the expressive old British language, the 'point to the left', as it looks like a tract almost cut off from the main land. It is much the richest in minerals; though at one time Kerrien was remarkable for its produce in this respect. The surface of both is healthy moorland, with little pleasant hollows here and there. In Penwith, eight or ten miles from Penzance, are the following places: The Guskus Mine, near St. Hilary; Wheal Darlington Mine, near Penzance; and the Alfred Mine, near Hayle. Wheal (or Huel) is the common name for a mine, and synonymous with the English *Wheel*, into which being worked on the joint stock or 'cost book' system, every shareholder puts a *spoke*, all directed to one centre. Treereiffe is the seat of the Le Grices; *Trengwainton*, of Mr. Davy. Near *Ludgvan*, (which was the rectory of Borlase, the county historian), is a large camp, 145 yards across. In the neighbourhood of Madron, or Maddern, are a pillar stone or two, and *Lanyon Cromlech*, which consists of a top stone or 'quoet', nearly 50 feet girth, resting on four other stones. St Buryan Church is a granite building, on a point of the moorland, 47 feet high; and it was once collegiate, and first founded by King Athelstone. Here too, are various curiosities, as the Merry Maidens, Boscawen-Oon, the Pipers, &c., generally styled 'Druid', but in many cases the result of natural causes. A Cromlech at Boskenna, near the Camp and Lamorna Cave. Boscawen-Oon is a circle of 19 stones, near the church, and gives name to the family of the Earl of Falmouth, one of whose members was the famous admiral. St Levan is close to the wild part of the coast. A little distance to the east is Treeren-Dinas, a camp in which stands the best *Logan Stone* (rocking stone) in Cornwall; it weighs 90 tons, but it is moved with a touch. One day in 1834 it was overturned by Lieut. Goldsmith and his crew, in consequence of a bet; but the people round were so highly indignant that he was compelled to replace it, which he did in a very ingenious manner, having, at the instance of Davies Gilbert, Esq., the President of the Royal Society,

The Logan Stone, said by Bradshaw to be the best rocking stone in Cornwall. 'It weighs 90 tons, but it is moved with a touch'. Note the man sitting beside the stone, giving an indication of its scale.

One final Brunel/Cornwall connection. Although the *Great Eastern* steamship was a failure as a passenger liner, it did have a very successful career laying telegraphic cables including one across the Atlantic in 1865. Cables from the continent came ashore at Porthcurno, near Land's End, and the display at the Telegraph Museum has a sectioned piece of the *Great Eastern's* cable.

obtained help from the Plymouth Dockyard. Tol Penden Penwith, as the extreme south point of the hundred is called, has a vast hole in the granite cliffs, through which the sea dashes up with a tremendous roar. A dangerous rock called the Rundlestone lies about one mile off it, marked by a buoy; and the dark Wolf-rock further out.

The effects of the Atlantic and the weather upon the hardest rocks (as granite is supposed to be) are visible all along this broken and disintegrated coast – a wild desolate region to the eye, but extremely healthful and inspiriting. Rare shells, sea weeds, and plants, should be looked for. The *Land's End*, the ancient *Antivestaeum*, is in St Sennen, the most westerly parish in England – being, in fact, in a line with Dublin and the Western Islands of Scotland. On one side of the village signpost are inscribed, 'The first Inn in England' (if you come from the west), and the other, 'The last Inn in England'. Sweetbriar grows here wild. Sennen Cove is a little creek in Whitsand Bay. Longships Reefs, half a mile long, has a lighthouse on it, 83 feet high. Some miles out are the Seven Stones light vessels. About twenty-five miles south-west are the Scilly Islands, a group of fifty or sixty granite islands and reefs, with an industrious population of 2,594. They belong to the Godolphin family. St Mary's is the largest. Here Sir Cloudesley Shovel, and four ships with 2,000 men were wrecked in a dreadful storm in 1707. A lighthouse has been fixed on St Agnes since the fearful event. Formerly there were fewer islands than at present, and it is said that a vast tract between them and the mainland was overwhelmed many centuries ago. That there is some truth in these traditions is evident from what we see going on at present time.

Michael Portillo with the author, John Christopher, at Paddington station in 2012 during filming for the *Great British Railway Journeys* television series.

More Bradshaw on Brunel from Amberley Publishing

Volume 2: Swindon to South Wales – published in February 2014
Volume 3: The Minor Lines – published in April 2014

Acknowledgements

I would like to acknowledge and thank the many individuals and organisations who have contributed to the production of this book. Unless otherwise stated all new photography is by the author. Additional images have come from a number of sources and I am grateful to the following: The US Library of Congress (*LoC*), Campbell McCutcheon (*CMcC*) and Gordon Collier. Final thanks go to my wife, Ute Christopher. Apologies to anyone left out unknowingly and any such errors brought to my attention will be corrected in subsequent editions. JC